# Inclusive Urban Design

# Inclusive Urban Design
## Streets for Life

**Elizabeth Burton**
**and**
**Lynne Mitchell**

AMSTERDAM • BOSTON • HEIDELBERG • LONDON • NEW YORK • OXFORD
PARIS • SAN DIEGO • SAN FRANCISCO • SINGAPORE • SYDNEY • TOKYO

Architectural Press is an imprint of Elsevier

Architectural Press is an imprint of Elsevier
Linacre House, Jordan Hill, Oxford OX2 8DP, UK
30 Corporate Drive, Suite 400, Burlington MA 01803, USA

First edition 2006

Notice
No responsibility is assumed by the publisher for any injury and/or damage to persons
or property as a matter of products liability, negligence or otherwise, or from any use
or operation of any methods, products, instructions or ideas contained in the material herein.
Because of rapid advances in the medical sciences, in particular, independent verification of
diagnoses and drug dosages should be made

**British Library Cataloguing in Publication Data**
A catalogue record for this book is available from the British Library

**Library of Congress Cataloguing in Publication Data**
A catalogue record for this book is available from the Library of Congress

ISBN 13: 9-78-0-75-066458-5
ISBN 10: 0-75-066458-4

For information on all Architectural Press publications visit
our website at www.books.elsevier.com

Typeset by Charon Tec Ltd., Chennai, India
www.charontec.com
Printed and bound in Great Britain

Working together to grow
libraries in developing countries

www.elsevier.com | www.bookaid.org | www.sabre.org

ELSEVIER     BOOK AID
             International     Sabre Foundation

To our inspiring mothers

Yvonne Burton and Irene Morgan

# Contents

# Foreword

There is a broad consensus about the optimal design features of buildings for people with dementia but the external environment has been neglected until recently. The research on which this book is based was a brave and rare attempt to fill this gap. This makes this book unique and especially important. People with dementia, and others with cognitive impairment, are constantly unnecessarily disabled by incomprehensible environments. We should do all we can to help them remain independent by giving due thought and attention to them. We do it for people with visual and hearing impairment and for those with mobility problems. It is time we addressed the needs of people with cognitive impairment so they can participate as fully as possible in society.

*Mary Marshall*
Retired Director of the
Dementia Services Development Centre
Stirling, Scotland

# Preface

This book represents the goals and spirit of our Wellbeing in Sustainable Environments (WISE) research unit. We formed WISE in 2004, within the Oxford Institute for Sustainable Development (OISD) at Oxford Brookes University. We wanted to give an identity to the research we had been doing for the previous 10 years, and to strengthen the basis for continuing it into the future.

Our objective at WISE is to investigate how the built environment (at all scales from buildings to whole cities) affects the wellbeing, health and quality of life of residents and other users. Our longer-term, more ambitious objective is to help bring about a change in the way we design our homes, streets, towns and cities. We believe sustainable development can only be achieved if the design professions fully accept their social responsibilities and make more use of evidence (from research and past experience) of user needs and how to address them. There is no reason why we cannot use a scientific approach (as other professions do) as the basis for creativity. It is becoming increasingly clear that built environments have profound influences on people's lives. We therefore need to know how to deliver maximum benefits.

Obtaining this knowledge is not an easy task, and we have only just begun to break the surface. Our research approach is novel because it seeks to identify individual design features that have a positive or negative effect on people's quality of life or wellbeing, and we have devised original methods and tools for doing this. We have developed ways of measuring built environments and investigating people's attitudes towards them. We always seek to generate practical guidance and recommendations. One of the reasons we have written this book is because so many people – mainly designers and producers of outdoor environments from all over the world – have contacted us to ask for our findings leaflets and design recommendations and for more information on designing dementia-friendly streets. We hope all the useful, relevant information is here, in one place, in an easy-to-use form.

Meanwhile, there is so much more research to be done, so much more we need to find out. We are constantly initiating new projects. We will attempt to disseminate new knowledge as effectively and swiftly as possible. We would be grateful for any feedback, comments or suggestions, and help in achieving the mission of WISE. We hope you enjoy this book, and, more importantly, we hope you can put our advice into practice.

*Elizabeth Burton and Lynne Mitchell*
WISE Research Unit, OISD

# The authors

**Elizabeth Burton MA (Cantab) DipArch DipUD PhD** is Postgraduate Research Tutor and Reader in the School of the Built Environment at Oxford Brookes University. She is also Director of the Wellbeing in Sustainable Environments (WISE) Research Unit in the Oxford Institute for Sustainable Development. After practising as an architect and urban designer, she has now been carrying out research on social sustainability and the built environment for over 10 years, and has won more than £750,000 in research grants from funders including the research councils, the Housing Corporation and NHS Estates.

**Lynne Mitchell MPhil MRTPI** is a Post Doctoral Researcher and Associate Postgraduate Research Tutor in the School of the Built Environment at Oxford Brookes University. She is a chartered town planner and her research interests lie in the relationships between social sustainability and the built environment. She is a co-founder and member of the Wellbeing in Sustainable Environments (WISE) Research Unit in the Oxford Institute for Sustainable Development.

# Acknowledgements

We would like to thank Shibu Raman for his important role in carrying out the research on which this book is based – we would not have been able to carry out the spatial analyses without him. We are also very grateful to Daniel Kozak, who kindly agreed to take most of the photographs and prepare the drawings to illustrate Streets for Life, while studying for his PhD degree. Our thanks go to the following, for contributing photographs:

> Carol Dair – Figure 1.3
> Kristina Stockdale Juhlberg – Figure 1.4
> Shibu Raman – Figures 2.5 and 4.7
> SURFACE Inclusive Design Research Centre, the University of Salford – Figures 5.3, 8.4, 8.6 and 9.7
> OPENspace, Edinburgh College of Art, Heriot-Watt University – Figure 11.1.

We are grateful to Mary Marshall, recently retired Director of the Dementia Services Development Centre, Stirling, for inspiring us with her enthusiasm and expertise, and we are grateful to our colleagues here in the Sustainable Urban Environments Group of the Oxford Institute for Sustainable Development (OISD) (especially Katie Williams and Carol Dair) for their ongoing support and encouragement.

Our research benefited from the advice and guidance of our steering group and findings group, including: Professor Tim Blackman; Susan Fairburn; Elizabeth King and staff at OPTIMA, Radcliffe Infirmary Trust; Joan King; Tom Owen; Maria Parsons and staff at the Oxford Dementia Centre; Diana Roberts; Dr Bart Sheehan; Dr Katie Williams; Professor Mike Jenks; Karl Kropf; and Steve Ongeri.

Finally, we want to thank our friends and family (especially Ben and Bart) who have been patient and encouraging during the process of writing the book.

# List of figures and tables

## FIGURES

## TABLE

# Structure of the book

The book is arranged into three parts. Part 1 (Streets for Life – Why?), containing Chapters 1–3, sets out the purpose and function of the book. It explains what the concept of Streets for Life means, why it has been developed, and how it fits with important issues in society today (Chapter 1). It also outlines the research from which the principles and recommendations for the concept were drawn (Chapter 1). Chapter 2 explains why it is important, in particular, to design for older people with dementia, outlining the predicted large increases in the numbers of people with dementia in the western world. Chapter 3 continues to focus on older people, explaining how they experience streets in their local neighbourhoods, how often, when and why they use them, and how they feel when they are out. This forms the basis for the following part of the book.

Part 2 (Streets for Life – How?), containing Chapters 4–9, is the main section of the book. This is where the principles and recommendations for designing Streets for Life are presented and explained. The recommendations are set out within the framework of six key design principles, with a chapter devoted to each:

- Familiarity (Chapter 4).
- Legibility (Chapter 5).
- Distinctiveness (Chapter 6).
- Accessibility (Chapter 7).
- Comfort (Chapter 8).
- Safety (Chapter 9).

Each chapter explains what is meant by the principle and how it affects older people and other users of neighbourhood streets. Then, we outline the aspects of street design that can contribute to achieving the principle, and, finally, present specific design recommendations.

Part 3 (Streets for Life – The Future?), containing Chapters 10 and 11, concludes the book by looking at implementation of the recommendations in practice, outlining potential barriers and possible further research (Chapter 10). Chapter 11 summarises the potential contribution of Streets for Life to UK towns and cities and beyond, to Europe and the rest of the world, explaining the significance and benefits of using the guidance.

We have designed the book so that readers can use the middle (Part 2) section for reference without having to read the rest of the book.

# PART I

# Streets for Life: Why?

# CHAPTER 1

# Origins of the Streets for Life concept

## THE MEANING AND USE OF THE CONCEPT

This book presents a new concept for design and development in towns and cities across the globe – 'Streets for Life'. We developed this concept through our ongoing research in the Wellbeing in Sustainable Environments (WISE) research unit in the Oxford Institute for Sustainable Development (OISD) at Oxford Brookes University. The unit is newly formed but is based on over 10 years' research looking at how the design of the built environment affects people's emotional wellbeing and quality of life. WISE research aims to offer design guidance, based on rigorous research investigating people's views and preferences, on creating environments that maximise people's quality of life. There has been so much interest in our Streets for Life design guidance, that we decided to include it all in this book, in a form that would be easy to read and use for those involved in the design and development of urban areas, neighbourhoods, streets and housing.

There are two main interpretations of Streets for Life:

1. Streets that residents find easy and enjoyable to use as they grow older in their neighbourhoods, allowing them to continue living at home if they want to.
2. Streets that are inclusive – they are easy and enjoyable to use by all members of society, including older people with dementia.

Through our research, we have begun to develop a set of design principles and accompanying design recommendations that we believe, if used, will enable designers and developers to create Streets for Life. This book is aimed at a range of people and groups, including:

- Producers of street environments:
  - Architects
  - Urban designers
  - Planners
  - Highways engineers
  - Access officers
  - Private developers
  - Housing associations
  - Manufacturers of street furniture.
- Users of street environments:
  - Older people and people with dementia
  - Carers of people with dementia
  - Groups representing older people and people with dementia
  - Anyone interested in their local environments and streets.

We recommend that the principles and recommendations be considered as early on in the development process as possible. They can be used in the development of whole new settlements, retirement villages or urban villages, regeneration and redevelopment of urban areas, development of private and social housing, or could be used to make improvements to any urban area without the need for a major development project.

## REASONS FOR DEVELOPMENT OF THE CONCEPT

### DEMENTIA PROJECT RESEARCH

In the WISE research unit, we are interested in designing environments to suit people of all ages and abilities. We are particularly interested in the relationships between built environments and mental health and cognitive impairment. It became clear to us that, although we are beginning to learn more about designing homes for people with cognitive impairments (e.g. smart homes), we know very little about designing outdoor environments. For this reason, we sought and won funding for a project on designing the outdoor environment for older people with dementia. We wanted to see how the environment could be designed to give these people as good a quality of life as possible. It is from this project that we developed the Streets for Life concept, and the recommendations in this book are all drawn from the findings of this project (Burton, Mitchell and Raman, 2004, Figure 1.1). None of the recommendations are the result of our professional opinions – they all stem directly from what people who use streets have told us, both those with and without dementia. We found a group of people from within Oxfordshire and Berkshire who were happy to contribute to the research – 20 with dementia and 25 without. We used three methods to find the answers to our questions. The key method was interviewing them in depth to find out how, why, and when they go out and what helps and hinders them when they do so.

A key message from the research was that it is invaluable for older people, especially those with dementia or memory problems, to be able to go out. Therefore we felt it was important for us to do as much as we could to promote the design of dementia-friendly neighbourhoods. We developed the Streets for Life concept as a mechanism for doing this.

### INCLUSIVE DESIGN

Streets for Life fit clearly within the concept of inclusive design. Inclusive design means designing products, services and environments that as many people as possible can use, regardless of age or ability. It is sometimes called universal design or design for all. It is not a new style of design but rather a new attitude or approach to design in general. Inclusive design has grown out of two major trends:

- The ageing of the population.
- The desire to bring disabled people into mainstream society.

By 2020, close to half the adult population of the UK will be over 50 years old, while 20 per cent of the US population and 25 per cent of the Japanese

Figure 1.1  The WISE dementia project findings leaflet (Burton, Mitchell and Raman, 2004).

population will be over 65 years. Ageing causes physical, mental and psychological changes. These often include multiple minor impairments in hearing, eyesight, dexterity, mobility and memory, which affect older people's ability to use products and environments with ease (these are addressed in more detail in Chapter 2). It is likely that as the baby boom generation ages, the older sectors of society will become increasingly vocal and demanding about the products, services and places they use. They are likely to have considerable wealth and high expectations for living active, independent and full lives, and will have significant market power to encourage designers and manufacturers to change their practices to address their needs.

A growing awareness of disability rights and burgeoning anti-discrimination legislation (including the US Americans with Disabilities Act 1990, the Australian Disability Discrimination Act 1992 and the UK Disability Discrimination Act, which was updated in 2005; see www.disability.gov.uk/law.html) has caused a shift in attitudes towards design for disability. In the past the emphasis was on adapting the person to fit the environment or on special design solutions or technology for disabled people. Now the 'social model' of disability is more common. Rather than seeing people as having disabilities, they are seen as being disabled by the environments and products provided for them. Those who adhere to the social model of disability aim to design environments and products to minimise 'disability' (Imrie, 2001; Lacey, 2004). It is seen to be important to design to meet the needs of everyone, or as many people as possible, rather than those of the 'average' fit, white, male, young adult (DfEE, 2001).

Accessibility has become a major issue because of campaigning by disabled people, the political influence of growing numbers of older people and more positive attitudes towards disability in general. Certain planning guidelines and building regulations aim to prevent or reduce the inaccessibility of buildings and transport for people regarded as having physical or sensory impairments, but there remain extensive problems with the scope, effectiveness and enforcement of these measures (Imrie and Kumar, 1998). Gant (1997), for example, documents the extent to which pedestrianisation over recent decades has positively transformed the accessibility of shopping centres for disabled people, but important shortcomings are evident such as the inadequacy of toilet facilities and a lack of clear signposting.

Imrie and Kumar (1998) draw upon the accounts of disabled people themselves to demonstrate the extent to which the built environment compounds their experiences of social and economic marginalisation. A common theme in the informants' accounts was to divide places between those that are safe and secure and those that are harmful and dangerous. It was often the home that was regarded as safe and secure, while the environment beyond the home was often perceived as harmful and dangerous. Humiliation was a frequent experience outside the home, such as having to access buildings by

**Figure 1.2** People are 'disabled' by the environments provided for them.

side or back doors or face high counters in offices and shops. A typical comment was, 'no one really gives a care about our needs *and we feel this every time we go outside*' (Imrie and Kumar, 1998, p. 366; emphasis added).

It is likely that inclusive design as a concept is here to stay. Various groups, including the Royal Society of Arts, RICAbility and the Design Council are campaigning for increased delivery of inclusive design, whether through new policy, guidance, standards, awards or training. A new British Standard on Inclusive Design Management, BS 7000-6, was published in January 2005. The Design Council website and the Royal Society of Arts website both contain an inclusive design resource (www.designcouncil.org.uk/inclusivedesignresource, www.rsa.org.uk/inclusivedesign).

Streets for Life are a natural extension of the inclusive design concept to the neighbourhood scale. The focus to date has been on products, buildings and physical access to buildings. Now it needs to broaden to whole neighbourhoods, villages and towns.

## LIFETIME HOMES

Perhaps one of the most well-known examples of inclusive design is the Lifetime Homes concept. We see Streets for Life as the outdoor or neighbourhood equivalent of this. The concept was developed by the Joseph Rowntree Foundation in 1991 (see www.jrf.org.uk/housingandcare/lifetimehomes), because of concern about the quality of British housing and lack of accessibility for older people, disabled people and those with young children (Brewerton and Darton, 1997). Lifetime Homes are homes that meet the needs of most households and the changing needs of households as they grow older. The Joseph Rowntree Foundation identified 16 design features that should be included in new housing (see www.jrf.org.uk/housingandcare/lifetimehomes/table2.asp for more details):

1. Parking space capable of widening to 3300 mm.
2. Distance from the car parking space to front door kept to a minimum.
3. Level or gently sloping approach to the Lifetime Home.
4. Accessible threshold, covered and lit.
5. Communal stairs provide easy access and, where homes are reached by a lift, it is fully wheelchair accessible.
6. Width of doors and hall allow wheelchair access.
7. Turning circles for wheelchair in ground floor living rooms.
8. Living (or family) room at entrance level.
9. Identified space for temporary entrance level bed.
10. Accessible entrance level WC plus opportunity for shower later.
11. Walls able to take adaptation.
12. Provision for a future stair lift.
13. Easy route for a hoist from bedroom to bathroom.
14. Bathroom planned to give side access to bath and WC.
15. Low window-sills.
16. Sockets, controls, etc. at a convenient height.

These design features are unobtrusive and easy to incorporate without incurring significant extra costs. Visually, or aesthetically, Lifetime Homes are not distinctive, but they offer many advantages to occupants because they allow flexibility and the ability to carry on living in them whatever their changes in circumstances and ability.

Lifetime Homes standards have now become mainstream. Many of them were adopted by the UK government when they extended Part M of the statutory Building Regulations in the mid-1990s to cover houses as well as public buildings (Carroll *et al.*, 1999). Others are included in the Housing Corporation's Scheme Development Standards, which all housing funded with Housing Corporation money must meet. Many clients and local authorities now require architects to adopt all the Lifetime Homes standards, and they are often viewed positively by developers as giving a marketing edge.

Streets for Life are 'Lifetime Streets' – streets and neighbourhoods that are easy to use and enjoy throughout a person's lifetime, whatever their changes in ability and mobility. For people to have a good quality of life in older age they need neighbourhoods as well as homes that they can use and enjoy. To provide this, we urge the use of Streets for Life recommendations alongside Lifetime Homes standards.

## SUSTAINABLE COMMUNITIES

Another spur for the promotion of Streets for Life has been the development of sustainability policies and the need for sustainable communities. Global concerns about impending environmental disaster (global warming, depletion of resources) from the late 1980s led to the development of a strategy for achieving sustainable development by the UK government (HM Government, 1994). This has gradually fed into sustainability policies in many different fields, but, as in the rest of the world, there has been a strong focus on the achievement of sustainability through land use planning and housing policies (Department of the Environment (DoE) and Department of Transport (DoT), 1994; DoE, 1996). In the 1990s, the government advocated the concept of the 'compact city' (i.e. the higher-density, mixed use city) through intensification of development in existing urban areas, including reuse of brownfield land and building new developments at high densities, close to transport nodes and facilities (Department of the Environment, Transport and the Regions (DETR), 1998; Burton, 2002). Compact city policies were later encapsulated within the concept of the 'urban renaissance' (Urban Task Force, 1999; DETR, 2000a). Through urban renaissance policies, the government intends to slow the well-publicised counter-urbanisation trends and encourage people back into towns and cities to new higher-density developments built on brownfield sites (DETR, 2000b).

**Figure 1.3** BedZED, Sutton: one of the new sustainable developments in the UK. (Photograph by Carol Dair.)

In February 2003, the Deputy Prime Minister launched the Communities Plan (Office of the Deputy Prime Minister (ODPM), 2003), establishing a £22 billion, long-term programme of action for delivering sustainable communities. The aims of the Plan are to encourage developments that offer a high quality of life to residents, and are places in which people want to live and to which they are proud to belong. The *Summit 2005: Delivering Sustainable Communities*, convened in Manchester, brought together more than 2000 experts to discuss the Plan and its implementation.

Sustainability has increasingly been accepted as being a balance of three elements (environmental, social and economic) and the emphasis has shifted from protection of the environment to improving the quality of life within the capacity of existing ecosystems (DETR, 1999). The policies are now in place, and architects and urban designers are being required to create 'sustainable settlements' and 'sustainable communities' (ODPM, 2003).

High quality design is clearly acknowledged in policy as a key component of a sustainable community. According to the UK government's PPS1 (Planning Policy Statement 1: delivering sustainable development, ODPM, 2005a):

*High quality design ensures usable, durable and acceptable places and is a key element in achieving sustainable development. (para. 33)*

PPG3 (Planning policy guidance 3: housing, DETR, 2000b) states:

*New housing and residential environments should be well designed and should make a significant contribution to promoting urban renaissance and improving the quality of life. (para. 1)*

But what is high-quality design? It is being promoted by many organisations, including the Housing Corporation, Commission for Architecture and the Built Environment (CABE) and the ODPM, who have produced design guidance documents (e.g. CABE, 2005). However, these contain mainly principles or objectives. For example, the joint DETR/CABE publication, *By Design – Urban Design in the Planning System: Towards Better Practice* (2000), endorses seven design principles, including 'a place with its own identity', 'a place where public and private spaces are clearly distinguished' and 'a place with attractive and successful outdoor areas'. Designers are told what a sustainable community should achieve (e.g. access to facilities, a mix of uses, attractiveness, safety, a sense of community and a healthy environment, ODPM, 2003), but what this means in practice is not yet clear. Some specific design guidance is available for particular principles (e.g. ensuring 'eyes on the street' to maximise feelings of safety), but much of the guidance is vague and difficult to apply. Higher-density housing can take many different forms, not only in terms of internal and external layouts and connections with surrounding areas, but also in terms of architectural style and detail, and arrangements of outdoor space and car parking.

Streets for Life contribute towards sustainable communities. A key aspect of social sustainability is social cohesion and social inclusion. Sustainable neighbourhoods should allow equality of access and opportunity, regardless of age or ability. The recommendations in this book go some way towards providing the much needed information and guidance on designing sustainable communities in practice.

## SUPPORTING THE INDEPENDENCE OF AN AGEING POPULATION

As mentioned earlier, the ageing of the population is increasing the need to design inclusively and encouraging product manufacturers and designers to take seriously the requirements of older people. It generates a number of reasons to adopt Streets for Life, not least because of the need to enable independence. The strain on public resources and lack of spaces in care and nursing homes mean that it is in the government's interest to enable people to stay living in their own homes for as long as possible. Over the past few years, the number of residential care homes for older people closing down has greatly exceeded the number established. Staying put is also usually what people want, and what is best for them, especially if they have dementia. But, to be able to do so, older people need not only homes that meet their needs, but also outdoor environments that they can use and enjoy. They need to be able to get out and about, otherwise they will be effectively trapped inside. As Hall and Imrie (1999, p. 424) state:

> The design and development of buildings and the built environment have the capacity to facilitate or to hinder people's movement and mobility, and particular designs ... are infused with powers of demarcation and exclusion.

Many older people live alone – they need to be able to get fresh air, exercise, go to the shops or post office, walk the dog, or meet up with friends. It is vital for their everyday existence, wellbeing and enjoyment of life.

Although there have been some advances in designing more accessible neighbourhoods for older people, the work so far has focused on physical or sensory needs rather than cognitive ones, in particular the needs of wheelchair users. By focusing on physical disabilities alone the disabling effects of the built environment on people with cognitive impairment are ignored, despite the definition of disability by the Disability Discrimination Act 1995 as a physical, sensory or mental condition. Research on designing the outside environment to meet the needs of older people is scarce compared to that for younger people with physical disabilities and non-existent for people with dementia (see Chapter 2 for more on this). There is a growing need to consider the implications of ageing in urban design. Streets for Life can enable older people, even those with dementia, to remain independent, living in their own homes, for longer. This has benefits for everyone.

**Figure 1.4**  A shortage of care home places makes it vital to enable older people to remain living in their own homes. (Photograph by Kristina Stockdale Juhlberg.)

## RESEARCH METHODS USED TO DEVELOP THE STREETS FOR LIFE CONCEPT

The study, which was funded by the Engineering and Physical Sciences Research Council (EPSRC), aimed to find out how to create dementia-friendly neighbourhoods that enhance and extend the active participation of older people with dementia in their local communities. The objectives of the study were as follows:

- To investigate how older people with dementia interact with the outdoor environment, the nature and quality of their experiences, and their understanding of the outdoor environment.
- To identify design factors that influence the ability of older people with dementia to successfully use the outdoor environment.

**Figure 1.5** If older people can get out and about in their local neighbourhoods, they are more likely to be able to remain living at home.

- To offer preliminary guidance (at all scales, from urban design to the design of street furniture) for designing dementia-friendly outdoor environments.

Forty-five ambulant people aged 60 years or over, living at home or in sheltered accommodation and still using the outdoor environment, participated in the research. Twenty were also in the mild to moderate stages of dementia, with a Mini-Mental State Examination score of between 8 and 20.

All participants were interviewed in depth to determine their perceptions and use of their local outdoor environment. They were shown sets of photographs of different aspects of the outdoor environment to find out their preferences in terms of design and reasons for liking or disliking particular features. The carer of each participant with dementia was interviewed at the same time, in a different room, to clarify details such as length of residence and whether the participant ever becomes lost. Many participants were also accompanied on short walks within their local neighbourhoods to record their wayfinding techniques and the environmental features that appear to help or hinder them. The design characteristics of participants' local neighbourhoods were measured in order to find out if they were related to the different quality of life outcomes for participants – for example, to see if those who reported positive feelings when outdoors were more likely to live in particular types of neighbourhood or urban forms.

We were interested in all aspects of the outdoor environment within people's local neighbourhoods, including the following:

■ Street network, shape and type
■ Open space
■ Junctions
■ Materials and kerbs
■ Street/footway widths
■ Street furniture, including seating and signage.

# CHAPTER 2

# The need for dementia-friendly streets

## AN AGEING POPULATION

This chapter explains why Streets for Life should be dementia-friendly. First, it looks at the worldwide phenomenon of the ageing of the population due to longer life expectancy and a reduction in birth rates. It then talks about the obligations of built-environment professionals to address the principles of inclusive design. This is followed by a brief synopsis of how the ageing process can affect people physically and mentally.

### WHAT DO WE MEAN BY 'OLD AGE'?

Any discussion of the needs and requirements of older people is hampered by a lack of consensus on when we actually become old. Should we follow the UK Office of National Statistics and Age Concern and refer to older people as those aged 50 years and over or should we copy the World Health Organisation and Help the Aged and use the age of 60 years as the start of old age? Fifty seems remarkably young and these days reaching 60 years is hardly noteworthy. We could use the term 'pensionable age' but this is complicated by the fact that in many countries women reach pensionable age at 60 years and men at 65 years. This discrepancy is in the process of being evened out; for example, 65 years will become the state pension age for everyone in Australia by 2012 and in the UK by 2020. But as it is being phased in over many years 'pensionable age' will be, at least temporarily, an even less useful means of denoting old age.

Many people, such as Laws (1994) and Norman (1987), have argued that using the term 'old' or attempting to identify an age by which time people should be regarded as being old is discriminatory and encourages a false distinction between the interests and needs of the younger population (stereotypically regarded as fit) and those of the older population (stereotypically regarded as frail). Yet for the majority of people the ageing process creates challenges that the design of the built environment currently does little to address or ameliorate. For the purpose of this book, we will use the term 'older people' to refer to people aged 60 years and over as this represents the age-span of our participant sample in the research described in Chapter 1.

## STATISTICALLY SPEAKING

There are currently 600 million people in the world aged 60 years and over. According to the World Health Organisation (2004), this is predicted to double by the year 2025, just 20 years away. In the European Union, 20 per cent of the population are 60 years of age or over and this is predicted to double by 2030 (Fabisch, 2003). Elsewhere, some countries are expected to experience more dramatic rises in the number of their older people than others. For example, the number of people aged 60 years or older in Thailand is predicted to rise from 8 per cent of the total population in 1999 to 30 per cent by 2050 while in Australia the number will rise from 16 per cent in 1999 to 28 per cent in 2050 and in the UK from 21 per cent to 31 per cent (United Nations, 1999).

However, an ageing population with a longer life expectancy and a reduction in birth rates now appears to be a worldwide phenomenon, except for certain parts of sub-Saharan Africa (Kalasa, 2001; Barnett Waddingham, 2002). In the UK, the 2001 Census found that, for the first time, there are now more people over the age of sixty than there are children. Even more remarkable is that the greatest increase is in the number of people aged 85 years and over (National Statistics Online, 2002).

## INCLUSIVE DESIGN

The built environment has traditionally been designed with the average young, healthy male in mind. We mentioned in Chapter 1 that although awareness that public environments should be made accessible to people with disabilities steadily increased over the last half of the twentieth century, design of the built environment to meet the needs of people with disabilities has generally concentrated on the accessibility needs of people with physical impairments, particularly wheelchair users, with a focus on the disability rather than on environmental barriers. While this has been, of course, a step in the right direction, it ignores the needs of a huge number of people with other types of impairment.

Until the design of the built environment takes into account the diverse needs of all users, many people will continue to be restricted or excluded from the outside world. Research has found that people in later life are often marginalised and discriminated against in comparison with younger adults (Help the Aged, 2005a; ODPM, 2005b). For example, despite the UK being the fourth richest country in the world, a third of our pensioners were living below the poverty line in the year 2000 (Help the Aged, 2005a). This marginalisation is often worse for people with dementia as Lubinski (1991, p. 142) points out:

> *Elderly individuals with dementia are amongst the most devalued members of our society, regardless of their lifelong characteristics and contribution. . . [the person with dementia] bears the double stigma of age and mental handicap.*

Disability is now legally defined in the UK Disability Discrimination Act (DDA) 2005 (which builds on the 1995 DDA) as a physical, sensory or mental condition. Similar laws exist in other countries, such as the US Americans with Disabilities Act (ADA) 1990 and the Australian Disability Discrimination Act (ADDA) 1992, which make it unlawful to discriminate against people with disabilities. Built-environment professionals and service providers in the UK have an obligation under DDA to make reasonable provision to ensure people can access and use premises, services and facilities regardless of disability, age or gender. Part M: *Access to and Use of Buildings* (2004 edition) of the Building Regulations 2000 sets out the requirements for achieving this. In the USA, Title III of the ADA contains the Code of Regulations for designing accessible public places and commercial facilities, *Standards for Accessible Design*, which was revised in 1994. This means that people of all ages with any form or level of impairment, whether it is a temporary injury (such as a broken limb), a major disability (such as blindness) or a cognitive problem (such as dyslexia) should not be excluded by environmental barriers. Members of the European Union are required by Mandate 283 (1999), to

**Figure 2.1**   Badly designed or maintained streets can be a problem for anyone but especially for older people.

make products and services available and accessible to users of all ages and abilities (Fabisch, 2003).

Many countries are attempting to improve the lives of marginalised people by introducing planning policies on inclusive design to produce places, services and products that are easy to use by everyone regardless of

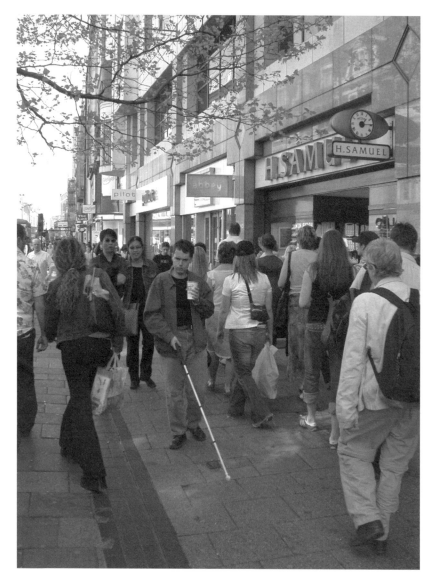

**Figure 2.2** Streets also need to accommodate the needs of younger people with physical, sensory or cognitive impairments.

age, ability or circumstances. In the UK, Planning Policy Statement 1: Delivering Sustainable Communities (ODPM, 2005a, para. 35) states that:

> *High quality and inclusive design should be the aim of all those involved in the development process. High quality and inclusive design should create well-mixed and integrated developments which avoid segregation . . .*

**Figure 2.3** Inclusive design addresses the needs of everyone.

*[and] create an environment where everyone can access and benefit from the full range of opportunities available to members of society.*

In England, housing associations that develop and manage social housing schemes also have to meet the requirements of their regulatory body, the Housing Corporation, which expects them to build sustainable communities by not only providing affordable dwellings but also ensuring that residents enjoy a good quality of life now and in the future. Their aim is to provide good quality housing situated in attractive, safe, clean environments, suitable for everyone including older people and people with disabilities, where they can easily reach schools, jobs, services, facilities and amenities (Housing Corporation, 2003).

The ageing process can cause people to experience any or all three of the types of conditions laid out in the UK DDA (2005). While not necessarily becoming severe enough to be defined as a disability, they will affect the ability of many older people to understand, use, enjoy and find their way around the outdoor environment. As Lavery *et al.* (1996, p. 189) state:

> *Designers must be aware of the fact that designing for the 'average' person is a thing of the past. The challenge of designing the 'Friendly Street' is a formidable one. The end product must not present a hazard to anyone: young or old, fit or frail.*

The challenge of making the outdoor environment accessible to people of all ages and capabilities may be a formidable one but there is now an obligation to make reasonable provision.

The following section explains the most common problems caused by the ageing process that are likely to affect the way older people experience and use the outdoor environment.

## THE AGEING PROCESS

It is a nonsense to assume that people within such a large age span of 60 years to, say, 100 years old will have the same needs and capabilities. 'Older' people are a heterogeneous group covering a wide range of ages, abilities, lifestyles, skills and mobility. Even if we try to separate them into subgroups of the younger old, the middle old and the older old the variations will be as great within each subgroup as between them (Laws, 1994). As Faletti (1984, p. 196) explains:

> *People do not age in the sense of experiencing diminished capacities in a homogenous fashion, nor do similar physical or mental changes necessarily reflect the same levels of reduced functional behaviour.*

In other words, reaching your 60th birthday does not herald a certain and steady decline into physical and mental incapacity. Neither does it mean that the desire for independence, choice and control over one's own life nor the need for social contact become any less important. Nevertheless, the ageing process can pose a number of physical and mental challenges that adversely affect people's functional abilities in a number of ways if the design of the built environment does not address these challenges. For example, around a third of people aged 65 years and over will fall at least once a year, rising to around half of those aged 85 years and over. Older people are also more likely to become injured by a fall than younger adults; in the UK, falls are the most common cause of death from injury in people aged over 75 years (Campbell, 2005).

**Figure 2.4**   How old is old?

## Physical Decline

Older people typically experience a decline in their strength and stamina, mobility and senses.

### 1. Strength and Stamina

People in their mid-70s generally have around half the strength and stamina of people in their 20s, which affects their ability to perform actions such as carrying, climbing, lifting, gripping, pulling and pushing (AIA, 1985; Carstens, 1985). As men are often around twice as strong as women, a man in his 20s could be four times as strong as a healthy woman in her 70s (Wylde, 1998).

### 2. Mobility

Many older people, especially those with dementia, develop a shuffling, unsteady gait and/or a stooped posture and look downwards when they walk so that they are less aware of their surroundings and potential hazards

(Carstens, 1985; Calkins, 1988). Bone and joint problems, such as arthritis and rheumatism, which affect people of all ages, reduce mobility and make people vulnerable to falls. Many older people cannot go up or down steep gradients or walk longer than around 10 min without a rest (AIA, 1985). So, for people with mobility problems even short trips around the local neighbourhood can become onerous expeditions if the streets are badly designed.

## 3. Sensory Impairment

People with sensory impairment are still able to absorb environmental information but require a greater reaction time and clear strong stimuli. Sensory impairments can include the following.

*(a) Hearing*: Some hearing loss is often the first major physical problem people experience as part of the ageing process, especially men. This reduces the ability to communicate, to understand what is happening and to hear and react to higher-frequency sounds, such as audible pedestrian-crossing signals. Hearing loss also makes it difficult to distinguish a particular voice or sound from general background noise, which can cause communication problems, confusion and disorientation (AIA, 1985; Carstens, 1985).

*(b) Vision*: While only a third of people in their 20s have problems with their eye-sight, sight naturally starts to deteriorate from around the ages of 40 to 50 years so that 98 per cent of people aged 65 years and older wear glasses. Around 10 per cent of people aged 65–75 years and 20 per cent of people aged 75 years and over have a more serious visual impairment, which is usually caused by a medical condition or disease rather than the ageing process. However, 90 per cent of blind and partially sighted people are aged over 60 years. People with visual impairments are far more likely than older people with good eyesight to fall over and to do so more than once (Campbell, 2005).
   Age related visual problems can include the following.

(i) *Diminished visual acuity*: People aged 40 years need twice as much light as 20 year olds and people over the age of 60 years need three to five times more light to achieve the same visual acuity (AIA, 1985; Brawley, 2001; Campbell, 2005). Declining visual acuity creates difficulties in seeing what is ahead, seeing things to the side, reading small print and distinguishing fine detail or faces, especially after the age of 70 years. The ability to switch between focusing on near and far objects also declines. People with poor visual acuity also have an increased sensitivity to glare and find it difficult to focus when moving between dark shadow and bright light. This can cause people to lose their balance, or to become disoriented or confused (AIA, 1985).

(ii) *Colour agnosia (reduced colour sensitivity)*: Colour agnosia is a reduced ability to distinguish colours caused by a yellowing of the lens of the eye as it ages. This condition is often aggravated by dementia. Dark colours and combinations of violets, blues and greens are the hardest to distinguish while reds and oranges remain the easiest to see. People with colour agnosia also find it difficult to distinguish soft pastel colours which blend into each other and to differentiate between colours of similar dark or light tones. Clear colours without any greyed or muted properties are more easily distinguishable but the most helpful characteristic for people with colour agnosia is clear colour contrast; for example, between floors and walls, on steps and edges and between symbols and backgrounds on signs (AIA, 1985; Harrington, 1993; Brawley, 1997).

(iii) *Impaired depth perception*:   Impaired depth perception causes people to misinterpret sharp colour contrasts or patterns on the ground as steps or holes. Deep shadows contrasting with light will also be seen as level changes. Shiny or reflective surfaces look wet and slippery and busy patterns, such as chessboard squares or repetitive lines can cause dizziness leading to trips and falls (AIA, 1985; Campbell, 2005).

### 4. Bowel and bladder weakness

Incontinence is not a normal part of the ageing process but the bowel and bladder do become weaker as people age so that older people generally need to use toilets more frequently than younger adults (Help the Aged, 2005b).

## Mental Decline

If people with physical incapacities find the outdoor environment difficult to negotiate and use, people experiencing mental decline are likely to find it even harder. Mental decline can be divided into general changes experienced during the ageing process and dementia.

### 1. General Decline

Research has found that as the brain ages, people tend to experience a change in their mental abilities. Although their mental abilities remain unimpaired it generally takes them longer to process, react to and recall information than when they were younger (AIA, 1985; Patoine and Mattoli, 2001). The types of memory that are commonly affected include 'semantic memory', which is the information we collect over the years through education and experience. Older people generally take longer to remember the names of people, places and objects or to learn new information than when they were younger. They also tend to need more time to complete mental tasks although they are still able to perform them as well as younger people. Many older people also have problems with 'prospective memory', which is the ability to remember tasks that need to be performed in the future, such as keeping an appointment or taking medicine and they often find that they rely more on lists and diaries than they did in the past. 'Procedural memory', however, which is necessary for skills such as swimming or playing an instrument, does not deteriorate providing those skills are regularly used (Twining, 1991; Huppert and Wilcock, 1997).

The term 'memory changes' rather than 'memory loss' is therefore perhaps a more accurate way of describing the affects of the ageing process on older people's mental faculties. To cope with these changes older people need to pay closer attention to new information they wish to remember. Stress, anxiety, tiredness, a lack of confidence or concentration, being distracted or in a hurry all have the potential to make it difficult to cope with these changes (Patoine and Mattoli, 2001).

Some physical ailments in older people, such as urinary infections, can cause temporary disorientation and short-term memory problems which cause people to fear that they might be developing dementia. People with visual or hearing loss are also sometimes wrongly thought to be developing dementia due to slower reaction times and misunderstanding what they have seen or heard (AIA, 1985; Twining, 1991; Barberger-Gateau and Fabrigoule, 1997).

## 2. Dementia

Dementia is the most common cause of permanent memory problems in older people (DSDC, 1995; Barberger-Gateau and Fabrigoule, 1997). The difference between general forgetfulness in old age and the memory problems experienced by people with dementia is that the former is typically a temporary struggle to recall inessential information while the latter represents a more permanent and dramatic loss of memory for important information and past experiences, along with other cognitive impairments (Reisberg *et al.*, 1986). Patoine and Mattoli (2001, p. 5) describe the difference between the two very succinctly:

> *Forgetting where you parked your car can happen to everyone occasionally, but forgetting what a car is may be cause for concern.*

We have already presented the figures for the predicted increase in the older population worldwide and noted that the biggest increase is currently in the 85 plus age group, at least in the UK. As there is a greater likelihood of developing dementia as one ages, the needs of an ever increasing number of people with dementia are becoming an urgent issue. While only one in 50 people have dementia between the ages of 65 and 70 years, this prevalence rises to 1 in 20 between the ages of 70 and 80 years, and 1 in 5 for people aged 80 years and above. In other words, 20 per cent of people aged 80 years and above have dementia. There are currently over 750,000 people with dementia in the UK and this is predicted to rise to about 870,000 by 2010 and over 1.8 million by 2050. Worldwide, there are nearly 18 million people with dementia and this is expected to increase to 34 million by 2025 (Alzheimer's Society, 2000).

Dementia is irreversible and incurable and generally follows a pattern of slow progressive cognitive decline accompanied by gradual and erratic

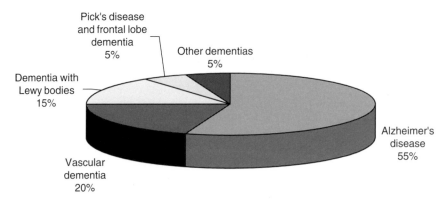

**Figure 2.5**   The main types of illness that cause dementia. (Chart by Shibu Raman.)

physical deterioration (Goldsmith, 1996; Perrin and May, 2000). It is not a disease in itself but can be caused by a number of illnesses, of which Alzheimer's disease is the most common and most well known, followed by vascular dementia, Lewy body disease, Pick's disease and frontal lobe dementia (Alzheimer's Society, 2000).

These illnesses can cause a number of cognitive, behavioural and personality changes. The majority of people with the more common forms of dementia – Alzheimer's disease, vascular dementia and dementia with Lewy bodies – first experience damage to the rear part of the brain causing cognitive changes, such as spatial and memory problems leaving the person confused and disoriented. Behavioural changes, such as an inability to cope with routine tasks, and personality or emotional changes, such as agitation, anxiety, depression and an acute sensitivity to surroundings, tend to occur at a later stage. The minority of people with frontal lobe dementia and Pick's disease initially demonstrate personality changes and loss of insight followed by orientation and memory problems. Despite these variations, 'for design, the differences are not as important as the similarities' (Calkins, 1988, p. 4). For most people, in the mild to moderate stages, long-term memory remains acute so that they can relate childhood events in detail but they cannot describe what they have done today. At the same time, people with dementia have to cope with the normal effects of the ageing process such as frailty, sensory impairment, poor mobility and reduced strength and stamina, which are often exacerbated by the dementia.

One of our participants was able to articulate his memory problems very clearly:

> *My short-term memories are much more fragile than my long-term memories. For example, if the cat disturbs me when I'm writing something*

*I forget what I was writing about. Recently, I put the teapot in the bedroom rather than the kitchen!*

As he is in the early stage of dementia he is still able to remember these inci-dences but as it progresses his ability to recall recent events and the names of things will diminish. A participant in the moderate stage of dementia tried to explain the frustration of diminishing abilities:

*I'm often learning a great deal about being old and this is one of the things that, you know, the way you lose . . . erm . . . oh um . . . to be able to get into your mouth what you know is somewhere here [tapped her head] and it's sort of disappeared. Oh dear!*

Another participant in the moderate stage of dementia demonstrated on the accompanied walk how she has lost the ability to put names to some types of buildings and features while still being able to articulate what they are used for. For example, she described a hospital as the place 'where people are ill', a block of flats as 'people live there but not in houses' and an underpass as 'where we can go underneath'.

In poorly designed environments, people with spatial orientation difficul-ties will struggle to understand their surroundings, to recognise where they are, to find their way around, to remember where they are going, to realise when they are lost or to relocate the correct route. Poor short-term memory retrieval further increases the chances of becoming lost through a reduced abil-ity to remember names, streets, places, alternative routes or directions. People with dementia can learn new information, such as their way around a new neighbourhood, but the information will never become an automatic memory and will require regular reinforcement by constant trips around the area.

During the early or mild stage, people generally retain the ability to cope independently and are usually able to get out and about successfully. In the moderate stage, some assistance is needed with activities of daily living, such as bathing and cooking. New medications to improve functional abilities in the mild to moderate stages, such as Aricept, Exelon and Rem-inyl, are enabling many people to live independently for longer, but they are not freely available. There are also a number of coping techniques which people can use to offset the difficulties posed by diminishing capabilities, such as keeping lists, following a set routine and sticking to familiar places (Patoine and Mattoli, 2001). Eventually, by the final stage of dementia, people have wide-spread brain damage resulting in a more generalised form of dementia and continual care is usually necessary (Alzheimer's Association, 2000).

## THERE'S NO PLACE LIKE HOME

Whether coping with the effects of dementia or just the normal ageing process, older people tend to experience a growing restriction of independence and lifestyle as capabilities decline and frailty increases. Many governments now promote care of older people in the community to enable them to stay in their own homes for as long as possible supported by social and health care services. Research shows that the majority of older people prefer to remain in their own home and that staying in a familiar home and neighbourhood becomes increasingly important to them as it helps to maintain a level of autonomy, privacy and stability at a time when they are likely to be coping with difficult changes in their lives (Axia *et al.*, 1991; Burley and Pollock, 1992; Laws, 1994; Marshall, 1998).

For people with dementia, 'following a regular routine in familiar surroundings' is even more essential (Patoine and Mattoli, 2001, p. 11). Around 80 per cent of people with dementia live at home, roughly a third of whom have severe dementia, and about a quarter live alone (DSDC, 1995; Audit Commission, 2000). Being moved from a familiar environment compounds their confusion and further reduces their ability to cope (Fogel, 1992; Goldsmith, 1996). Baragwanath (1997) found that moving people with dementia to unfamiliar environments, such as respite homes or hospitals, caused them so much anxiety and disorientation that they were more likely to injure themselves than in their own homes. The predictable and reliable nature of a familiar environment is less likely to cause confusion and stress and remaining in the familiar home environment also enables people with dementia to maintain some control over their own lives and a network of friends and neighbours. As Fogel (1992, p. 16) says, 'for the more impaired, remaining at home may have the additional significance of being the one constant in an emotional world threatened by losses'. It is, therefore, important to make sure that the design needs of people with dementia are met if they are to live at home successfully but we would all benefit from a dementia-friendly environment that is easy to use and understand.

Even when the decision is made to move into residential care, a major problem is that supply is not keeping up with demand. Privatisation of residential care for older people in the UK heralded an initial increase in provision but over the past few years the number of care homes that have closed down has greatly exceeded the number of new ones that have been established. The UK lost 13,100 residential care places in 2001, another 13,400 by April 2003 and a further 9600 by April 2004 (Laing and Buisson, 2005). Unless a great deal of investment is committed soon, this situation will worsen as the population ages and the number of people with dementia increases correspondingly.

Too often it is taken for granted that people with failing capacities endure a poorer quality of life than before. Help the Aged (2005c) claim that

**Figure 2.6** If streets are not designed to meet the needs of older people many, especially those who are frail or have dementia, will be effectively trapped in their own homes.

a million older people have reported feeling trapped in their own homes yet the positive effects of fresh air and exercise, social interaction and even just being out on the street amongst people should not be underestimated. Lifetime Homes (described in Chapter 1) and Smart Home schemes which equip people's homes with assistive technology, such as detectors that remind the resident to turn the gas off or alert a central response unit when a person falls, provide safe, easy to use indoor environments. But unless people can also safely and effectively get out and about in the locality many will become housebound, especially those with mental impairments such as dementia.

People with dementia particularly need regular mental and physical exercise to keep their minds and bodies active. Regardless of the reasons why it is difficult to get out of the house, the resulting increase in physical frailty, social isolation, low self-esteem and loss of independence can be debilitating both physically and psychologically. As Robson (1982, p. 265) states:

> *Even if it [going outdoors] is only routine activity, it may be vital for their quality of life, and even for them to maintain any independence and self-respect.*

In the next chapter we show how important it is to the participants of our research to be able to go outdoors.

# CHAPTER 3

# Older people's experiences of their local streets

## INTRODUCTION

This chapter presents findings from our dementia research project (described in Chapter 1) on older people's general experiences of their local neighbourhood streets. It includes data for older people with and without dementia, comparing the two groups. In seeking to offer guidance on designing streets that are suitable for older people, it is important to first understand how they engage with streets, when and why they use them and what their concerns are in terms of design.

## HOW, WHEN AND WHY OLDER PEOPLE USE THEIR LOCAL STREETS

We were surprised by how many and how often older people, with or without dementia, go out. This was partly because, of course, we only interviewed older people with dementia who still go out at least occasionally. But most of the participants with dementia and all of those without dementia go out alone, over half in each group daily.

We asked the participants to tell us where they usually go. The top destinations for those with and without dementia (in descending order) are as follows:

| Older people with dementia | Percentage of participants | Older people without dementia | Percentage of participants |
|---|---|---|---|
| Shops | 95 | Shops | 100 |
| Post office | 85 | GP surgery | 92 |
| Nowhere in particular | 70 | Post office | 80 |
| Visiting friends | 45 | Church | 68 |
| GP surgery | 40 | Nowhere in particular | 68 |
| Visiting family | 35 | Visiting friends | 56 |
| Park | 25 | Park | 36 |
| Church | 15 | Visiting family | 24 |

For both groups, shopping is the most common destination for trips – almost all our participants go shopping. Going to the post office is also a regular destination. It is clear that the majority of older people also regularly go out for its own sake, without having a particular purpose or destination in mind.

About half the participants regularly visit friends. Fewer visit family, probably because they are less likely to be living nearby. Nearly half (40 per cent) of those with dementia and some (20 per cent) without dementia said they have family living locally, while well over half (60 per cent) of those with dementia and nearly all (92 per cent) of those without dementia have friends living nearby. Many of those who do not visit said that friends and family come to them, as it is easier.

There are two clear differences between those with and without dementia in terms of where they go:

1. Participants with dementia tend to avoid socially demanding situations, such as visiting friends or attending church, preferring simple activities such as going to the corner shop or posting a letter.
2. Participants with dementia are significantly less likely than those without dementia to visit more than one place in a single trip (25 per cent of people with dementia, and 88 per cent of those without, visit more than one place in a trip).

Participants with dementia are far more physically restricted in their independent use of the outdoor environment than those without dementia. As they no longer drive or use public transport unaccompanied their choice of destination is limited to within walking distance of home.

**Figure 3.1** Almost all older people, with or without dementia, regularly go shopping.

## HOW OLDER PEOPLE FEEL WHEN USING THEIR LOCAL STREETS

Our research showed that older people experience a variety of emotions when they go out, and can feel different on different days. However, it was clear that the majority enjoy the experience, both those with and without dementia. Enjoyment was the most commonly reported feeling when out in the local neighbourhood (60 per cent of both those with and without dementia reported feeling this). Participants also commonly reported feeling happy (15 per cent of those with dementia, 12 per cent of those without), comfortable (40 per cent with dementia, 12 per cent without) and safe (15 per cent with dementia, 16 per cent without). The quotes below reflect these positive feelings:

> *'I feel great. I would live out!'*
> *'I enjoy going out – I feel ugh if I don't!'*
> *'I get claustrophobic if I don't go out'*
> *'I like going out'*
> *'I rejoice!'*
> *'It's lovely being like we are now, you know, able to come out of our home and come out into this nice place and have either a long walk or just a little . . . little . . . tootle around and then home again. It's very comforting.'*

Although negative feelings were less common, the participants did report feeling:

- Anxious
- Fearful
- Bored
- Intimidated (especially people with dementia, in formal spaces with imposing architecture)
- Confused
- Embarrassed (particularly when getting lost)
- Lonely.

The most common negative feeling was one of anxiety or fearfulness. Some are anxious about being out at night or in unfamiliar places. Many people are afraid of going out because of physical problems such as unsteadiness or poor eyesight. They fear falling over or being knocked over by cyclists, skateboarders or people 'barging into them'. They discussed the difficulties presented by uneven paving, poor seating, bicycles on footpaths and steep inclines. They also referred to social and psychological difficulties, such as the closure of local shops, poor bus services and the fear of attack or of getting lost.

Getting lost seemed to provoke different feelings in different people. For some it was very scary: one participant said 'It was extremely spooky to me; my hair went on end because I was actually lost', whereas for others it is more a feeling of embarrassment, for example, one commented 'I was a bit of a Charlie!'. Many older people like going out for its own sake whereas others were adamant that they only like going out if there is a good reason or purpose for doing so.

The key differences in feelings between older people with and without dementia are:

1. In interviews, those with dementia were far less likely than those without to say that they face any problems when they are out.
2. The few with dementia who did refer to problems focused on physical impairments, such as an unsteady gait or poor eyesight. Findings from the accompanied walks showed that people with dementia do face similar problems to those described by participants without dementia but are less aware of them.
3. On the accompanied walks, none of the participants without dementia showed signs of anxiety, confusion or fear. However, around half those with dementia were anxious or confused when they were unsure of the route or distracted by sudden noises.

## HOW OLDER PEOPLE READ THE STREET ENVIRONMENT

When interviewed, fewer participants with dementia said that they sometimes lose their way than those without dementia; however, carers confirmed that a higher number of participants with dementia get lost. On the accompanied walks, none of the people without dementia and one-third of participants with dementia lost the way.

People with dementia often struggle to interpret the cues that signal the use of buildings, the location of entrances, the behaviour that is expected in different places or the intentions of people around them. The participants with dementia are able to understand places, streets, buildings and features that are in designs recognisable to them. It appears that style (whether traditional or modern) is less important than clarity of function and use. They also continue to remember features that they encounter on a regular basis.

**Figure 3.2**   Older people with dementia struggle to understand buildings that do not make their purpose obvious.

## BENEFITS OF USING LOCAL STREETS

We found that going out is of huge importance to many older people, for a whole range of different reasons. There appear to be five key benefits.

### FREEDOM AND AUTONOMY

The participants made comments such as 'I feel in charge of myself' and 'The world belongs to me just for that bit of time', which show just how important being able to get out into the local streets and neighbourhood is for many older people, especially those with dementia. For many, it is the only time they feel really in control of their own lives at a time when they are losing many of the abilities they have taken for granted for so long: they can often choose where they want to go and manage the trip successfully from start to end.

### DIGNITY AND SENSE OF WORTH

The older people we interviewed expressed to us how important it was to be able to do something useful, even if it was something as small as posting a letter, buying the newspaper or walking the dog. The ageing process can be a humiliating and degrading experience, especially for those who develop dementia, and can cause people to lose their sense of worth, value and self esteem. Going out and using local streets to accomplish simple tasks contributes in a significant way towards restoring older people's sense of worth.

### FRESH AIR AND EXERCISE (PHYSICAL HEALTH)

Some of the older people we talked to like to go out mainly for fresh air and exercise. For example, one participant said 'I love walking and I always feel better for getting out and getting a bit of fresh air'. This was often the case for people who tended to go out for its own sake rather than to accomplish particular tasks. Our researchers were sometimes surprised by the energy and enthusiasm of those taking part in the accompanied walks – participants were encouraged to decide themselves where and how far they wanted to go, and walks ended up taking as long as 2 hours, sometimes over stiles and across fields.

Fresh air and exercise, of course, has knock-on effects on physical health and mental wellbeing.

### PSYCHOLOGICAL WELLBEING AND ENJOYMENT (MENTAL HEALTH)

A very important benefit of going out and walking the local streets is simply one of enjoyment, which contributes to general happiness and wellbeing.

**Figure 3.3**   Being able to accomplish a simple task is a huge boost to the self-esteem of people with dementia.

One participant enthused, 'It's really quite a warm sun this, isn't it, do you feel it? It's delicious'. Levels of depression are relatively high among older people living in care homes – part of this may be their loss of ability to go out in the local area. There is a huge appreciation of nature, trees, plants and wildlife among older people. It was obvious on the accompanied walks that many older people notice these aspects of their environment. Some use trees and planting as cues for wayfinding. There is often an appreciation of buildings

**Figure 3.4**   Older people benefit in a variety of ways from fresh air and exercise.

and architecture too. Older people use landmarks such as churches and towers to find their way around.

## SOCIAL INTERACTION

One of our interviewees commented, 'It's nice to meet people we know in the street and stop for a chat'. Going out provides many points of contact for older people, not just through planned trips to visit friends and family, but through informal interactions with neighbours on the street, shopkeepers and other people enjoying recreation in parks and other open spaces.

**Figure 3.5** Older people particularly enjoy seeing greenery and trees in their neighbourhoods.

Contact might be a chat or just a greeting or smile, but this can make a huge difference to people, especially those who live on their own, giving them real contact with the outside world.

Social interaction has been shown to be good for mental health as well as general wellbeing. It is a central part of people's quality of life.

**Figure 3.6** Being able to go out gives older people the opportunity to meet others.

## COMMON PROBLEMS AND DESIGN CONCERNS

We asked participants in the research to tell us any problems they face when they go out. Their responses fell into five different categories (in descending order of frequency):

| Problem | Percentage of comments |
|---|---|
| No problems | 40 |
| Difficulties walking | 25 |
| Fear of falling | 23 |
| Difficulties crossing roads | 10 |
| Fear of getting lost | 02 |

Almost half the participants could not identify any problems at all, but of those who could, difficulties walking and fear of falling were by far their main concerns. Difficulties walking were seen to stem from their own impairments and disabilities, but also from steep slopes and steps in the local neighbourhood. Some people felt the problem is because shops, bus stops and facilities are too far away or because there are not enough public seats for resting en route. The fear of falling again stems partly from personal impairments such as poor eyesight or general frailty, but participants also identified uneven or slippery surfaces, cyclists on pavements, road/pavement works and lack of dropped kerbs as causes. Crossing roads is seen to be made more difficult by dangerous, speeding or heavy traffic, and crossings not being in the right places.

We also asked how participants thought the outdoor environment could be improved. They had lots of interesting, useful ideas and views on this. Their suggestions could be divided into the following categories (in descending order):

| Suggestion for improvement | Percentage of comments |
|---|---|
| More or clearer signs | 14 |
| Better maintained pavements | 14 |
| More safe crossings/crossing points | 10 |
| More seats | 09 |
| No obstructions (e.g. building materials, parked cars) blocking pavements | 07 |
| Better bus stops/shelters | 06 |
| Fewer or better level changes (e.g. handrails on slopes) | 05 |
| Smooth surfaces (no slabs or cobbles) | 03 |
| More or better litter bins | 03 |
| More or better marked dropped kerbs | 03 |

(Continued)

**Figure 3.7** A common fear for older people is that uneven or damaged surfaces will cause them to fall.

| Suggestion for improvement | Percentage of comments |
|---|---|
| More toilets | 03 |
| Slowed traffic (calming measures) | 03 |
| Variety of buildings and interesting features | 02 |
| No bicycles on pavements | 02 |
| More local facilities/bus stops | 02 |
| Wider pavements | 01 |
| Clearer figures and sounds at pelican crossings | 01 |
| More lighting | 01 |
| No suggestions | 09 |

**Figure 3.8** The most commonly offered suggestion for improving local streets was to have clearer signs – this sign is difficult for older people to read because the graphics are too small and it is too high.

Maintenance of pavements, including repairing broken paving slabs and cutting back overgrown hedges is obviously a major concern of older people, though not one that designers can do very much about, apart from to design low or easy maintenance streets. The key concerns that can be addressed at the design stage are the provision of clear signs, crossings and seats.

# PART II

# Streets for Life: How?

# INTRODUCTION TO PART 2

This book is predicated on two simple facts: first, that everyone ages and, second, that people of all ages benefit from design that helps older people to use, understand, enjoy and find their way around their local streets. In other words, by creating environments that even older people with dementia can use effectively our streets and public places really will be for life.

In Part 2 we explain what we consider to be the reasonable and necessary requirements for making Streets for Life. Our findings are based on preliminary research in an area that to date has been neglected. They show that there are six key design principles: streets need to be familiar, legible, distinctive, accessible, comfortable and safe.

Chapters 4–9 discuss each of these principles in turn. Each chapter begins with a brief definition of the principle it is addressing and then explains how this affects older people's ability to use and enjoy their local neighbourhoods. Each chapter then outlines the aspects of street design that can help to achieve the principle in question and lists specific design recommendations. It is important to note that the principles are interdependent and share some common characteristics and recommendations.

# CHAPTER 4

# Familiarity

## WHY FAMILIARITY IS AN ESSENTIAL CHARACTERISTIC OF STREETS FOR LIFE

### WHAT DO WE MEAN BY FAMILIARITY?

Familiarity refers to the extent to which streets are recognisable to older people and easily understood by them. Familiar streets are hierarchical and long established with forms, open spaces, buildings and features in designs familiar to older people.

### HOW FAMILIARITY AFFECTS OLDER USERS OF THE OUTDOOR ENVIRONMENT

#### Recognising Where They Are

Most environments conform to certain design patterns and people tend to develop general expectations of how particular places are laid out and what they contain. For example, on entering a supermarket people would normally expect to see rows of shelving containing food and household items for sale and a line of checkout tills. If these expectations are not met it can be very confusing and disorienting (Zimring and Gross, 1991). Guidance on

**Figure 4.1**   People have a general expectation of what they will find on main streets.

designing the internal environments of care homes stresses the important role familiar settings play in preventing and alleviating disorientation and confusion. Such guidance typically promotes the design of small, domestic-style care homes that provide a more familiar and understandable living environment than institutional or hospital-style settings. Bedrooms, bathrooms and living areas designed to resemble those found in older people's own homes in terms of size, layout, décor, furniture and furnishings are used to help residents understand where they are and what is expected of them in each room or part of the care unit. This, in turn, helps to reduce levels of frustration and anxiety. For further information on design guidance for dementia-friendly indoor environments please refer to Mitchell *et al.* (2003).

**Figure 4.2**    People also have a general expectation of what they will find on side streets.

In Chapter 2 we discussed the significance of a familiar home environment in reducing confusion and helping older people with dementia to maintain their independence. Familiar outdoor environments and features that older people recognise and understand are just as influential, especially for those experiencing spatial disorientation, confusion and memory problems. For example, people generally expect cities and towns to have a centre, perhaps with a public square or monument or memorial. High streets are usually wide, busy with traffic and pedestrians, and lined by buildings at least two to three storeys in height with shops on the ground floor and offices or flats on the upper floors. Side streets are generally expected to be narrower, quieter and more residential. When neighbourhoods conform to these expectations they provide familiar, predictable and understandable environments, which help people to recognise where they are and what is expected of them in that setting.

For most people, the longer they live in one place the more familiar they will become with their neighbourhood and all its individual components of urban form, street layout, the choice of alternative routes, the location of services, facilities, pedestrian crossings and street furniture and so on. None of the participants with dementia in our research now drive and most are reluctant to use public transport unless accompanied. This means that they are left with a limited choice of destinations within close walking distance of home. Although this adversely affects the general quality of life of those living in poorly designed neighbourhoods, most of our participants, with and without dementia, attribute their ability to find their way around to the fact that they rarely go further than their local neighbourhood or diversify from a regular, small set of routes and destinations. A participant with dementia explained that 'I'm just used to the area. I've got to know it and I go to the same places more or less each time'. On the accompanied walks this was confirmed by the fact that attempting to follow a less familiar route was one of the main causes of participants losing their way.

Our research also found, however, that for people experiencing short-term memory problems, the ability to recognise and remember the neighbourhood has to be constantly reinforced by walking along the same streets and encountering the same architectural and environmental features on a regular basis. The participants with dementia also generally seem less aware of changes in their local neighbourhood than those without dementia and when they do notice a change they are more likely to become confused or disoriented by the experience.

## Understanding Their Surroundings

Just as people have expectations of what different types of places should normally look like, they also have a general idea of the visual images of different building usages, such as shops, offices and houses. When designs follow these familiar visual styles people can understand them even on their first visit but if ambiguous or unfamiliar designs are used this will not be the case. For example, it used to be traditional for buildings to face onto the street with the main entrance clearly visible at the front but modern buildings often face away from the street so that pedestrians are met by a blank façade with little clue as to what the building is for or how to get into it. People with dementia particularly find it difficult to 'read' the nature and use of different spaces if their identity is ambiguous. This can cause them to mistakenly enter private places or be reluctant to use public places.

Research into the design of dementia care facilities has found that people with dementia often do not recognise more modernistic designs or

**Figure 4.3**   Many modern buildings present a blank façade to pedestrians with little cues as to their identity or how to get into them.

they misinterpret their usage. For example, many will no longer be able to understand how to use sliding or revolving doors because they do not swing open on hinges like more familiar and commonly encountered 'normal' doors. People with dementia are also likely to presume that glass doors are windows (American Institute of Architects (AIA), 1985).

In our research, a number of participants with dementia failed to recognise modern designs of street furniture, such as telephone kiosks, bus shelters and public benches and the majority of those who could identify them still prefer street furniture in traditional styles. Public telephone boxes are a good illustration of this point. The traditional red K6 telephone box is the most popular type of public telephone with our participants for two reasons. First, because of its long-term familiarity; as one participant with dementia put it, 'It's familiar – I've known it all my life and it exudes cosiness'. This was echoed by many participants without dementia including one who said,

**Figure 4.4** People with dementia often do not recognise modernistic designs or they misinterpret their usage.

'I prefer this one because it's familiar. I've used them before'. Second, K6 telephone boxes are the most popular type because their function is obvious; as a participant with dementia said, 'it's familiar and functional and doesn't pretend to be anything else but a telephone box'. It is interesting to note that many modern telephone boxes and kiosks display ambiguous text and symbols rather than the simple and straightforward word 'telephone' displayed on the K6.

The most important factor here is not just that older people prefer traditional designs because of their familiarity or aesthetic appeal but also that older people with dementia often cannot identify what the modern types actually are and older people without dementia often avoid using more modern features because they fear that they will not understand how to use them.

During the research we considered whether symbols would be a useful alternative form of sign for people with dementia. However, when we showed the participants a photograph of a tourist information sign the majority, both with and without dementia, told us that they had not encountered such a sign before. Many struggled to understand what it represents. Those with dementia made comments such as 'I haven't got a clue' and 'What on earth is that? I've never seen one'. Only one participant with dementia attempted to work out what it might mean although with little success, for she said, 'And what might that be? It might mean "ideas". Any ideas?' A number of the participants without dementia were just as dismissive of its unfamiliarity; for example, one participant told us that 'it doesn't tell me a thing. I don't know it'. However, a number of participants without dementia were able to identify its meaning even if they thought they had not seen one before; for example, one asked, 'I don't really know what it is, is it "information"'? It is, of course, probable that many of the participants have seen the tourist information sign without taking any notice of it as it is not a necessary part of their daily lives but it demonstrates that if symbols are both unfamiliar and ambiguous they are of little use to older people.

We also showed the participants a photograph of a barber shop pole. We found that the people without dementia recognised the pole and what it represents, as one participant said, 'that's a barber's sign – no doubt about that'. However, very few participants with dementia were able to identify it and two people, rather frighteningly, thought they indicated road crossings, with one asking, 'I can't remember anymore what this is. Is it something to do with a street crossing?' This is a good illustration of one of the major findings of our research that people with dementia only remember even familiar places, streets, buildings and environmental features if they encounter them on a regular basis. Barber shop poles are not often used these days, as one participant without dementia pointed out, 'the younger generation probably do not know what that means' and so will not be seen regularly enough for people with dementia to be able to reinforce their memory of them. Another

**Figure 4.5** Most people are familiar with the traditional red K6 telephone box but, just in case, it also has the word 'telephone' in large clear graphics on all four sides.

**Figure 4.6** This modern telephone box presents a confusing array of unfamiliar signs and symbols.

**Figure 4.7** The tourist information sign – 'any ideas?' (Photograph by Shibu Raman.)

interesting finding here is that people with dementia are less likely or able to try to make sense of the unfamiliar so that features such as symbols must be clear and unambiguous and in styles familiar to older people to be of any practical use. Signs are dealt with in more detail in Chapter 5.

# HOW CAN FAMILIARITY BE ACHIEVED?

## ASPECTS AND FACTORS OF THE OUTDOOR ENVIRONMENT THAT HELP TO CREATE FAMILIARITY

### Streets

It is important for long-established streets to be maintained and any change should be small-scale and incremental. Enhancing the existing built environment is preferable to large-scale re-development which is more likely to cause disorientation, confusion and anxiety in older people, especially those who are less aware of their environment and rely on constant reinforcement. In new developments the use of local forms, styles and materials will help older people to become familiar with the new neighbourhood.

Maintaining or designing a hierarchy of familiar types of street, from high streets and side streets to lanes and passageways gives a clear overall image of an area and what each type of street is likely to offer.

### Architectural and Environmental Features

Public buildings and main entrances should be clearly visible from the street and in designs that older people can recognise and understand. Architectural features, such as doors and windows, in local styles and materials can help to achieve this. We are not suggesting that only traditional designs and styles should be used; adhering only to traditional designs would be rather monotonous and would rule out the large number of modern designs that play an essential role in inclusive design. Sliding doors, for example, are an invaluable help to wheelchair users, people pushing prams or buggies, people loaded down with heavy bags, people with little strength and many more, but providing both hinged and sliding doors is ideal. The important thing is to make sure that features are familiar, unintimidating and easy for older people to understand; combining familiar and long-established designs with the necessary aids to accessibility would make them more inclusive to older people. Continuing with the example of telephone boxes, it would surely be relatively easy to merge the familiar style of the K6 red telephone box with the flush threshold and easier to open door of the modern boxes. This is in line with government advice:

> There is also a danger of seeing the detailed design response as either 'traditional' or 'modern'. Such debates about style can get in the way of producing a distinctive quality response to the design challenges involved. Traditional materials and design ideas can be used in a totally modern

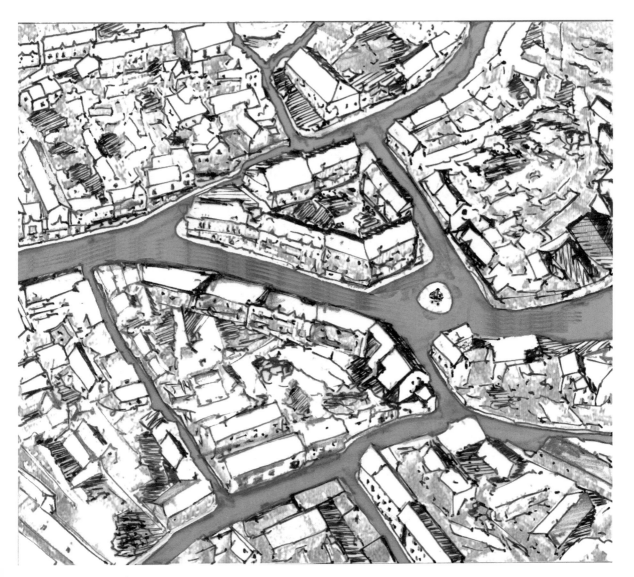

## Hierarchy of street types

**Figure 4.8**    A hierarchy of familiar types of streets gives a clear image of an area. (Drawing by Daniel Kozak.)

*way. Conversely, new materials and cutting-edge construction technologies can be deployed to create a comfortable human-scale architecture and, where appropriate, reflect traditional styles.* (Department of Transport, Local Government and the Regions (DTLR), 2001, p. 74)

## DESIGN FEATURES AND CHARACTERISTICS OF FAMILIAR STREETS FOR LIFE

Familiar Streets for Life are likely to be places where:

- Streets, open spaces and buildings are long established.
- Any change is small scale and incremental.
- New developments incorporate local forms, styles, colours and materials.
- There is a hierarchy of street types, including main streets, side streets, lanes and footpaths.
- Places and buildings are in designs familiar to or easily understood by older people.
- Architectural features and street furniture are in designs familiar to or easily understood by older people.

# 5

# Legibility

## WHY LEGIBILITY IS AN ESSENTIAL CHARACTERISTIC OF STREETS FOR LIFE

### WHAT DO WE MEAN BY LEGIBILITY?

Legibility refers to the extent to which streets help older people to understand where they are and to identify which way they need to go. Legible streets have an easy to understand network of routes and junctions with simple, explicit signs and visible, unambiguous features.

### HOW LEGIBILITY AFFECTS OLDER USERS OF THE OUTDOOR ENVIRONMENT

#### Finding the Way

Apart from our research presented in this book, there have been few studies on the wayfinding and orientation abilities of older people in the outside environment and none of people with dementia. Up until now research has tended to be conducted in laboratories, despite the fact that such findings have been found to be conflicting and do not necessarily give a clear picture of people's abilities in the real world (Cornell *et al.*, 1999; Kitchin, 2000). Studies that have observed older people's wayfinding techniques in real settings, such as those by Passini *et al.* (1998, 2000) and Wilkniss *et al.* (1997) focus almost exclusively on the indoor environment.

We discussed in Chapter 4 how participants tend to attribute their successful wayfinding to the fact that they now restrict their activities to the local neighbourhood. However, we found that most of the participants, with and without dementia, also use some form of wayfinding technique, although this is often a sub-conscious activity.

### 1. Maps and Directions

Very few participants with wayfinding problems use maps or written directions to find their way round their local neighbourhoods. Most of the participants with and without dementia commented that they are finding maps increasingly difficult to understand and follow as they grow older. A participant without dementia told us that 'I've really lost the knack of maps'. When shown a map of their local neighbourhood many found it difficult to locate their home or to show us their proposed route for the accompanied walk. This caused anxiety for some, including a participant with dementia who exclaimed, 'Oh, look at that map, it's … it would worry me!'

Some participants are willing to ask for directions when they are out but this was not seen as a particularly helpful tactic. They are either doubtful that they would be given reliable or understandable information or worried that they would not be able to remember or follow the directions.

### 2. Mental Maps

A number of participants, with and without dementia, said that they visualise a mental image of their route as they walk along. Their descriptions of how they do this were many and varied, including 'I sort of imagine it as I go along', 'I carry a map in my mind' and 'I picture the roads and houses I'll be passing'. However, as we found that those with dementia are less likely to be aware of changes in their local streets, it is difficult to know how accurate their mental maps now are.

### 3. Route Planning

Our participants tend to visit a small number of destinations in their local neighbourhoods and to follow the same route on each trip; for example, one participant with dementia said, 'If I want to go the post office it's go out of the front door and turn right and if I want to go to the doctor's surgery I go out and turn left'. However, many told us that they plan their journey ahead of time, especially if there is more than one possible route they can take. Some also remind themselves of the landmarks they will be passing; a participant without dementia explained that 'I think about which way to take; for example, I think, "go past the bridge and cut over at the gravel pits"'.

It is interesting that those who talked about using mental maps and route planning techniques are also those who told us that they sometimes lose the way. Whether they are more aware of their problems or are simply happier to admit to having difficulties, a legible neighbourhood would mean that less conscious effort is required to prevent them from losing the way and that they would be less fearful of getting lost.

### 4. Signs

Participants had strong views on the use and design of signs in the outdoor environment and those with dementia find them increasingly difficult to cope with. They struggle to interpret the information supplied by signs and will sometimes follow the instructions regardless of where they actually want to go or what they want to do. Participants who lost their way on the accompanied walks were far less able to name buildings, streets and places, sometimes even when signs giving their names were apparent.

**Figure 5.1**   Symbols must be as clear and realistic as possible.

Participants find clusters of signs difficult to read because they are too cluttered, and signs crowded with information too complicated to make sense of. They also find signs with abbreviations or stylised graphics difficult to understand. As we explained in Chapter 4 stylised signs are not familiar enough to older people and are generally too ambiguous to be easily interpreted. Even the relatively clear bicycle symbol painted on cycle lanes was not recognised by everyone, including some people without dementia. In fact, one participant with dementia wondered if it was a picture of a pair of spectacles!

**Figure 5.2**   Multiple pointers can be ambiguous and the graphics too difficult to read.

Signs too low to the ground can be obliterated by obstructions such as stationary vehicles and those high up are often too small to read. The pedestrian post and multiple pointers are treated with suspicion as 'they can be confusing which way they are pointing and kids turn them round'. Participants also criticised the size of the graphics on this type of sign and the contrast between the colour of the graphics and the background colour as being difficult to read.

A-frame boards are considered to be of little practical use especially if there are 'too many blooming boards' creating 'too much clutter so it's not possible to read any of it'. They are also criticised for blocking the pavement causing a dangerous hazard as they walk down the street. 'You are here' signs were also criticised by many of our participants with dementia for being 'too complicated', 'confused' and 'a jumble'. Some of those without dementia also admitted to finding them too complicated and a number also told us that they find that the graphics are too small for them to read.

Participants with and without dementia prefer simple, straightforward signs on single pointers, either on posts or fixed perpendicular to the wall. The post office sign is a particularly good example of a sign that is popular with older people as it is well established, familiar and encountered regularly. The colour scheme is also very good for older people with colour agnosia (see Chapter 2) as colours on the red/orange spectrum tend to be the last colours to be lost. However, it would be preferable if the lettering was in red and the background in the lighter orange colour.

### 5. Landmarks and Environmental Features

Few people stated in interviews that they use landmarks and environmental cues, by which we mean the distinctive natural and built features of a particular environment. However, we found during the accompanied walks that the majority look for both distant and nearby landmarks and other environmental features to help them to know where they are and which way they need to go even though they are not always aware of doing so. On the accompanied walks most of those who lost the way were able to relocate the correct route on their own by retracing their steps and looking for familiar landmarks, such as the corner shop, and identifying environmental features, such as a letterbox or favourite tree.

### Losing the Way

During the interviews we were surprised to be told by the majority of people with dementia that they never lose their way. However, through interviewing the carers and going on the accompanied walks we found that many of the participants with dementia do have problems finding their way around. A common response to the question 'Do you ever find that you lose your way?' was

**Figure 5.3** The UK Post Office sign, a particularly dementia-friendly sign. (Photograph by SURFACE Inclusive Design Research Centre.)

'Oh no, my dear, I never get lost'. Yet many carers told us about distressing occasions of scouring the streets when the person they cared for was hours late returning home. Some had even had to call for police assistance. It is difficult to know whether these participants were reluctant to admit to having problems or whether they had actually forgotten losing the way because of their poor short-term memory. On the accompanied walks, a third of participants with dementia lost their way. None of those without dementia had any difficulties finding their way around, including those who had told us that they sometimes do have wayfinding problems.

Quite a few participants without dementia talked about how they sometimes lose their way by making the wrong turn at decision points, such as road junctions and crossings or when leaving a building or bus. Many also mentioned becoming disoriented after a period of daydreaming or 'going on auto-pilot' as they walk along. Indeed, a common cause of disorientation and confusion during the accompanied walks was a break in concentration caused by being distracted. There were many causes for this, such as chatting too much, as a participant with dementia suddenly told us, 'I've been talking so much that I've allowed myself to get lost, actually'. Other distractions include being startled by a sudden loud noise such as an emergency vehicle siren or someone shouting, and being faced with excessive visual stimuli or information, such as a clutter of signs.

An interesting finding of our research is that the people who lost the way during the accompanied walks all live in neighbourhoods with complex street layouts with few connecting streets, such as housing estates made up of a number of culs-de-sac. A lack of direct routes can be very disorienting. We mentioned in Chapter 4 that trying to follow a less familiar route was one of the causes of participants losing the way. However, even on more familiar streets, one of the most common places where they became disoriented was at road crossings and junctions where they had to make a decision about which way to turn. Road crossings and junctions are particularly difficult when there are a number of visually similar routes to choose from or where it is difficult to see along each street. This corresponds with the experiences related to us by participants without dementia in the interviews.

Being able to see the end of a short street was noted by many as helpful to them; for example, we were told, 'I like to see my path through' and 'it would be easier to locate a house on a short one'. Most participants also prefer gently winding streets to long, straight streets. Explanations as to why this is included 'the bends and twists are more interesting', 'there's more variation' and 'it gives a change of scenery'. This also helps to maintain concentration, which is necessary to avoid becoming disoriented or confused. Relatively narrow streets also help people to concentrate due to the closer proximity of environmental cues as well as feeling 'cosier' and less threatening than wide streets.

**Figure 5.4**   Junctions with a number of routes to choose from can be very disorienting especially if the streets are difficult to distinguish from each other.

For older people, fear of getting lost can be a reason for becoming
housebound. Lynch (1960, p. 4) understood how frightening being lost or
disoriented can be for anybody:

> *To become completely lost is perhaps a rather rare experience for most people
> in the modern city. We are supported by the presence of others and by
> special wayfinding devices: maps, street numbers, route signs, bus plac-
> ards. But let the mishap of disorientation once occur, and the sense of anx-
> iety and even terror that accompanies it reveals to us how closely it is
> linked to our sense of balance and well-being.*

This experience is even worse for people coping with frailty, poor mobility or
cognitive impairments. For those with spatial disorientation and short-term

**Figure 5.5** The markings on this junction seem designed to help drivers but not pedestrians.

memory problems each trip around the local neighbourhood can be a journey into the unknown. If they are also unable to seek help or to follow directions an illegible environment is extremely debilitating.

# HOW CAN LEGIBILITY BE ACHIEVED?

## ASPECTS AND FACTORS OF THE OUTDOOR ENVIRONMENT THAT HELP TO CREATE LEGIBILITY

### Street Layouts

The most legible street layout for older people, especially those with dementia, are streets laid out on a deformed or irregular grid. The irregular grid creates a more interesting overall street pattern, provides direct, connected routes which are easy to understand and gives people a clearer view ahead than the 90° turns and blind bends created by uniform grids. It also means that forked, staggered and T-junctions can be used, rather than cross-roads,

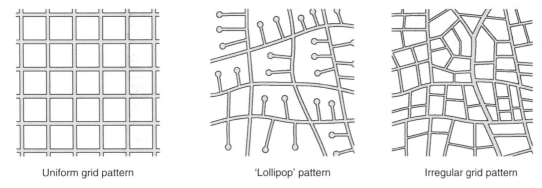

Uniform grid pattern      'Lollipop' pattern      Irregular grid pattern

**Figure 5.6** Although the uniform grid provides a pattern of well-connected streets the layout of identical streets and cross-roads can be as confusing as the 'lollipop' pattern. The irregular grid pattern also has small perimeter blocks and connected streets but creates a variety of block and street shapes. (Drawing by Daniel Kozak.)

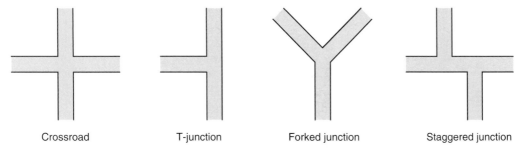

Crossroad      T-junction      Forked junction      Staggered junction

**Figure 5.7** Forked, staggered and T-junctions reduce the number of routes to choose from and provide a focus point at the end of the street. (Drawing by Daniel Kozak.)

**Figure 5.8**  Fairly narrow streets with gentle bends are generally more interesting to walk along than wide, straight streets.

which keep the number of alternative routes to a minimum and provide a focal point at the end of the streets. In Chapter 4 we recommend having a hierarchy of street types that older people are familiar with. In terms of legibility the hierarchy also helps them to know where they are.

## Street Shape and Size

Street blocks should be of varying short lengths from around 60–100 m to allow for variety. The longer streets should be gently winding to break up the length and to provide slowly emerging views as people walk along. Streets should also, preferably, be relatively narrow to help maintain concentration.

## Public and Private Space

The edges of the street blocks should be lined with buildings facing the street. In Chapter 4 we explained how familiarity can be enhanced by having buildings fronting the street because this is what older people are more used to. In terms of legibility, buildings facing the street help to provide a visually interesting street frontage and a clear distinction between public and private space. We also referred to the fact that people with dementia struggle to understand what places and buildings are for and may enter private property by mistake. Public spaces and buildings should give a clear image of what they are for and make their entrances obvious. Physical boundaries, such as fencing, walls and hedges, can also help to differentiate public from private space. It is important, however, to keep them low so that the buildings or spaces behind them and their entrances, architectural features, building numbers and names can still be seen.

## Signs

Barker and Fraser's 1999 guide to inclusive signage is a useful source of information on the specifications required to make signs accessible to people with disabilities and, therefore, all users. However, in summary, the best signs for older people are plain and simple and provide explicit, essential information only. They should have large, non-stylised dark lettering on a light background and symbols should be realistic and unambiguous. Signs should also have non-glare lighting and non-reflective coverings.

Signs giving directions should preferably be on posts and single pointers and positioned at important wayfinding decision points, such as road junctions and crossings. Signs identifying the location of a place or building are most effective when perpendicular to the wall as they can be seen from a distance but as too many on one street would be confusing they should be restricted to essential shops, services and facilities. Signs positioned flush on a wall, such as those identifying the name of a place or building, should be in a clear contrasting colour to that of the wall. Signs fixed to walls, rather than on free-standing poles, also help to reduce street clutter. As older people often find maps difficult to interpret, 'You are here' signs are not particularly useful to them but will be appreciated by other people, especially people unfamiliar with a place providing the graphics are of an adequate size and colour contrast to the map.

## Landmarks and Environmental Features

Distinctive landmarks and environmental cues are discussed in detail in Chapter 6. The most important factor in terms of legibility is that long established landmarks are retained and that street furniture, in designs familiar to older people, and other latent cues, such as trees, are positioned at decision points and where the line of sight ends.

**Figure 5.9**  A legible street. The buildings face the street and have low boundaries to delineate private space without blocking the view. The T-junction provides buildings to focus on at the end of the street rather than a further stretch of road and a minimal choice of routes. Trees and a post box on the street corner act as useful wayfinding cues.

## DESIGN FEATURES AND CHARACTERISTICS OF LEGIBLE STREETS FOR LIFE

Legible Streets for Life are likely to have:

- A hierarchy of street types
- Blocks laid out on an irregular grid based on an adapted perimeter block pattern
- Small street blocks of varying lengths from around 60–100 m
- Well-connected streets

- Gently winding streets with open ended bends and corners greater than 90°
- Short, fairly narrow streets
- Forked, staggered and T-junctions rather than cross-roads
- Places and buildings with clearly visible, obvious and unambiguous functions and entrances
- Low walls, fences and hedges and open fencing separating private and public space
- Minimal signs giving simple, essential and unambiguous information at decision points
- Directional signs on single pointers
- Locational signs for primary services positioned perpendicular to the wall
- Signs with large, realistic graphics and symbols in clear colour contrast to the background, generally with dark lettering on a light background
- Signs with non-glare lighting and non-reflective coverings
- Street furniture and other latent cues positioned at decision points and where visual access ends.

As already mentioned, the six characteristics are all inter-related but legibility is particularly related to distinctiveness which is discussed in Chapter 6.

# 6

# Distinctiveness

## WHY DISTINCTIVENESS IS AN ESSENTIAL CHARACTERISTIC OF STREETS FOR LIFE

### WHAT DO WE MEAN BY DISTINCTIVENESS?

Distinctiveness relates to the extent to which streets give a clear image of where they are, what their uses are and where they lead. Distinctive streets reflect the local character of the area and have a variety of uses, built form, features, colours and materials that give the streets and buildings their own identity within the overall character of the neighbourhood.

### HOW DISTINCTIVENESS AFFECTS OLDER USERS OF THE OUTDOOR ENVIRONMENT

#### Knowing Where They Are

In Chapter 4 we discussed the importance of retaining familiar, well established places, streets and features. As well as enhancing familiarity, local character gives a neighbourhood its own distinctive identity, which further helps older people to understand where they are and to feel at home in their surroundings.

## Maintaining Concentration

People of all ages do not always simply choose the most obvious route to reach their destination; they are also influenced by how interesting or dull each route is (Llewelyn-Davies, 2000). On the accompanied walks, most of the participants, particularly those with dementia, chose uncomplicated routes with more variety of land use, building form and architectural features even though they were not the shortest route. Explanations for choosing these routes included, 'I prefer the variation in architecture', 'it's got more character about it' and 'it's more interesting and colourful'. Mixed use streets, and places with buildings and architectural features in a variety of local styles, sizes, shapes, materials and colours not only make a neighbourhood more interesting to walk around but also help people with dementia to maintain concentration.

Participants tend to perceive uniform uses and designs as 'very boring' and lacking in the distinctive features necessary for identifying where they are and which way they need to go. As a participant with dementia said of a photograph of a row of identical houses, 'I don't like this because they are all the same – I would get the houses mixed up'. Streets that are identical to each other in terms of shape and layout or are lined with identical buildings with few distinguishing features can cause anyone to experience disorientation and confusion.

We also found that those with dementia prefer to visit smaller, more informal or 'natural' green open spaces, such as wooded areas, rather than formal settings, such as botanical or historic gardens. The people without dementia tend to appreciate both types. The participants with dementia also tend to prefer parks full of areas of activity, such as tennis courts, children's play areas, boating ponds and so on and small, urban squares with shops and cafes and useful, interesting or pleasant features, such as seating, public art and greenery. Explanations for these preferences included 'there is more variety' and 'it is much more interesting . . . it would be unlikely that I'd get lost'. The more vibrant, mixed use spaces provide the necessary interest and stimulation for people who need to maintain concentration to avoid losing the way.

## Feeling a Sense of Belonging

People with dementia often struggle to interpret the intentions of people around them or the behaviour that is expected in different places and worry that they may fail to behave appropriately. We found that the participants with dementia tend to stick to relatively easy activities, such as visiting the local shops, posting a letter or taking the dog for a walk and are far less likely than those without dementia to be involved in more socially demanding activities, such as going to the library, a place of worship or a social club (see Chapter 3).

**Figure 6.1** Older people with dementia tend to prefer informal urban open spaces to empty, formal squares.

In Chapters 4 and 5 we discussed how older people with dementia find it difficult to identify the use of buildings and places unless their designs are explicit. The participants with dementia are not, in general, keen on visiting formal urban squares, which tend to have empty expanses of ground surrounded by large, imposing buildings. Participants explained that they were not keen on formal open spaces because 'nothing's going on' and 'a lot of these lovely old buildings are a lot alike so you can't always be sure what you're looking at'. Participants with dementia are concerned that such places 'seem to be more official' so they would not be certain whether they are public or private spaces and that they would feel like an intruder. Many of the participants without dementia appreciate the attractiveness of the architecture in formal squares but still have their reservations about their formality, size and emptiness.

## Finding the Way

Current urban design guidance promotes the use of civic and distinctive landmarks:

> *Landmarks such as distinctive buildings, particularly those of civic status, towers or statues help provide reference points and emphasise the hierarchy of a place.* (Llewelyn-Davies, 2000, p. 61)

These are particularly useful for older people. In a comparative study on the ability of younger and older adults to learn new landmarks, Lipman (1991) found that the older participants remembered fewer new landmarks than the younger adults and organised them according to their distinctiveness rather than their sequential order.

In Chapter 5 we referred to the fact that few participants stated in interviews that they use wayfinding cues, such as landmarks and cues, but the accompanied walks demonstrated that the majority use both distant and nearby landmarks and other environmental features to help them to clarify their location and route. As a participant without dementia told us as we walked along, 'I think one likes to see landmarks passing by so that I am sure that I am progressing'.

We found that the participants regularly use five different types of landmarks and two types of environmental features.

### 1. Landmarks

*(a) Historic buildings and structures:* Historic buildings, such as churches, and historic structures, such as memorials and monuments, are particularly important as they are more likely to be remembered due to having been in existence for a very long time. On the accompanied walks, many participants pointed out historic landmarks that they find distinctive and interesting; for example, a participant without dementia said, 'there you can see Consuela's memorial and the tap's still behind the seat'.

*(b) Civic buildings:* Civic buildings, including town halls, hospitals, village halls and libraries are also important landmarks, as described by a participant

**Figure 6.2** Historic buildings make good landmarks as they are generally notice-able and interesting pieces of architecture and are more likely to be remembered as they have been in existence for a long time.

without dementia, 'I have landmarks, for example, Welcome Hall then left to Sainsbury's'.

*(c) Distinctive structures:* Distinctive structures, including high-rise buildings, bridges, spires, steeples and towers were often pointed out to us on the accompanied walks, such as 'Do you see that steeple? That's on our block of flats' and 'Thames Valley police have their headquarters there – you probably saw a lot of flagpoles'.

*(d) Places of interest and activity:* We have already referred to the fact that people with dementia tend to prefer to visit places of informal activity

**Figure 6.3**  Distinctive structures catch the eye and help people to identify which way they need to go.

rather than those that are more formal or deserted. We also found that many participants, especially those with dementia, use places such as parks, commons, playing fields, tennis courts, nature reserves, allotments, play areas and recreation grounds as landmarks.

*(e) Unusual places, buildings or usages:*  Unusual places, buildings or usages that have a distinctive local identity, such as 'the toothpaste tube houses', 'the witch's gingerbread house' and 'the big ugly house at the end' were used during the accompanied walks to identify where we were or which way we needed to go.

## 2. Environmental Features

Moore (1991) found that environmental cues are first recognised in terms of their function, followed by their location and then their architectural style or character. He also notes that they are recognised most quickly when they are in familiar or well-organised environments or when they are in familiar, easy

**Figure 6.4**   A practical feature that is also distinctive and attractive.

to understand styles. Our findings from the accompanied walks confirmed this and we also found that the participants routinely use two main types of environmental features as orientation and wayfinding cues:

*(a) Aesthetic features:*   Aesthetic features, such as water pumps, fountains, village greens, ponds, attractive front gardens, trees, hanging baskets and flower tubs, were used on the accompanied walks to identify the direction we

**Figure 6.5**   Familiar street furniture and aesthetic features positioned on street corners provide distinctive wayfinding cues.

were going in and the location of our destination; for example, a participant without dementia explained to us that 'the post office is just about as far as the trees on that side'.

*(b) Practical features:* Practical features, such as street furniture including red telephone and letter boxes, public seating and bus shelters, were used in the same way as aesthetic features. Comments were as varied as 'there are no good landmarks so I might look for different curtains in front windows' and 'these are the humps up Mill Street, you see? We're about to come to my favourite pub'.

Landmarks and environmental features are often used in conjunction with each other; for example, a participant with dementia explained to us that 'there's a road goes down from the top down towards the park and then you can go down that way and under the bridge and go up to the shops that way'. Participants most often use these wayfinding cues when they are positioned at the end of their field of vision and at decision points, such as road junctions, to focus on. Again this is a common wayfinding tool in all age groups. Golledge (1991) found that people make fewer mistakes when such 'anchor points' are positioned at places where complex decisions are required. Temporary or obscure structures have little usefulness as landmarks regardless of their distinctiveness, so environmental features need to be long-term and in unambiguous styles. Taking one step at a time and looking for familiar, distinctive features along the way helps older people to identify where they are and which way they need to go next. This is particularly the case for people with mild to moderate dementia for other studies have found that as their ability to find their way around complex layouts diminishes, they continue to be able to find their way if they break their journey up into sections by moving from one familiar and visible cue to the next (Passini *et al.*, 1998). However, it is important to remember that we also found that people experiencing short-term memory problems have to constantly reinforce their memory of routes and wayfinding cues by regularly walking along the same streets and encountering the same features.

Many of the participants in the mild stage of dementia have the insight to realise that their memory and orientation capabilities are deteriorating and are making a conscious effort to remember environmental wayfinding cues to ensure they are able to continue to go out into their local neighbourhoods. One participant constantly reminds herself of the number of lamp-posts from her house to the correct turning for the newsagent. Another participant has taught himself to recognise a friend's house by the fact that his roof tiles are a different colour to those on the neighbouring buildings. Other participants do not make such conscious efforts but are nevertheless guided by a number of environmental cues; for example, one participant pointed out a tree that her husband had planted on a triangle of grass at a road junction in their village years ago. She could no longer remember why he had planted the tree but its distinctiveness, its position at a decision point and its personal significance means that she always recognises it and knows where she is when she comes to it.

Participants also use distinctive or individual features to help them to locate or identify their own home. Descriptions include 'my house is the only one with wooden cladding in the street', 'I look for my fence as it's the only one' and 'there is nothing like our house, it's so distinctive'. This demonstrates the importance of having the variety of building form mentioned earlier.

## HOW CAN DISTINCTIVENESS BE ACHIEVED?

### ASPECTS AND FACTORS OF THE OUTDOOR ENVIRONMENT THAT HELP TO CREATE DISTINCTIVENESS

### Local Character

As we have already recommended in Chapter 4, new developments should reflect the local character of the surrounding areas. Any infill or regeneration of an existing place should blend in with the local character and existing built form. This does not mean that new developments and buildings should be carbon copies indistinguishable from their neighbours. A variety of local architectural designs, materials and colours should be used to give them their own distinctive identity while maintaining the local character of the neighbourhood. As we discussed in Chapter 4, neither does this mean that modern architectural designs should not be used; they can become important landmarks in their own right. The important goals are to make sure that new designs complement, rather than detract from, the surrounding local traditional designs so that the area retains its distinctive local identity and the designs provide clear, unambiguous and understandable signals as to the building's identity, use and entrances.

### Varied Urban and Building Form

In Chapter 5 we talked about the irregular grid pattern being the most legible layout for older people. In terms of distinctiveness it allows for more variety of shapes and sizes of streets and junctions. A mixture of uses and building forms with different shapes, features, materials, colours and contrasts, such as varying roof lines, tiles and chimney pots, gables and balconies and a variety of porches, front doors, windows and gardens are all useful tools for helping people to know where they are by making each street distinctive from their neighbours without losing the local character of the whole area. Lynch (1960) was advocating the need to make streets distinctly identifiable by their individual design, materials, colours, lighting, boundaries, vegetation and skyline 45 years ago. Yet

**Figure 6.6** Gently winding streets with varied form and features are more interesting than straight uniform streets.

an astonishing number of identical, uniform streets were built in many countries during the last part of the twentieth century.

## Interesting, Understandable Places

Places and open spaces need to provide distinctive cues to their identity so that it is clear what they are used for and whether they are public or private. Urban squares and green spaces should be small and informal with plenty of activity, delineated footpaths and a variety of features, such as seating, trees and other soft landscaping. We are not advocating the removal of all formal open spaces; for one thing, this would be completely against our recommendation of retaining local character and distinctive landmarks. However, such spaces could be made more welcoming by clarifying where people are allowed to go through the use of footpaths and seating, and the introduction of some soft landscaping.

**Figure 6.7**  People with dementia find it difficult to maintain concentration when walking along straight uniform streets.

## Landmarks and Environmental Features

As we described earlier, there are five major types of landmarks that are the most useful and commonly used by older people. Retaining or establishing these types of landmarks will help to produce distinctive Streets for Life:

1. Historic buildings, such as churches, and historic structures, such as memorials and monuments.
2. Civic buildings, including town halls, hospitals, churches, village halls and libraries.

**Figure 6.8** A skittles green in a Barcelona park – a popular place of activity and a useful wayfinding cue.

3. Distinctive structures, including high-rise buildings, bridges, spires, steeples and towers.
4. Places of interest and activity, including parks, commons, playing fields, tennis courts, nature reserves, allotments, play areas and recreation grounds.
5. Unusual places, buildings or usages that have a distinctive local identity.

There are also two main categories of environmental features that help to produce distinctive streets for life:

1. Aesthetic features, such as water pumps, fountains, ponds, attractive front gardens, trees, hanging baskets and flower tubs.
2. Practical features, such as street furniture including red telephone and letter boxes, public seating and bus shelters.

These environmental features are particularly useful wayfinding cues when they are positioned at junctions and street corners. They are also excellent cues when placed on long streets where they can be seen from the entrances to the street. Apart from their distinctiveness, the most important characteristic of the landmarks used by older people is that they are either noticeable or interesting structures or places. The main attribute of the environmental features is that their designs or features are easily recognisable. Both types of wayfinding cues, however, are only remembered by people with dementia if they are encountered on a regular basis so that temporary buildings, structures and features are not useful as wayfinding cues.

In summary, it is important that, wherever possible, well-established historic, civic and distinctive landmarks and places of activity should be preserved. The legibility of public areas can also be improved by the use and strategic positioning of street furniture, trees, flower tubs, hanging baskets and public art providing they are allowed to remain in the same place for a substantial period of time and are not so numerous as to cause an excess of external stimuli and street clutter. Permanently fixed street furniture will also be of far more value as wayfinding cues to people with visual impairments than landmarks, no matter how distinctive they might be.

## DESIGN FEATURES AND CHARACTERISTICS OF DISTINCTIVE STREETS FOR LIFE

Distinctive Streets for Life are likely to have:

- Local character.
- Varied urban and building form.
- Small, informal, welcoming and understandable local open spaces with varied activities and features.
- A variety of open spaces, such as public squares, 'village greens', allotments and parks.
- Streets, places, buildings and architectural features in a variety of local styles, colours and materials.
- A variety of historic, civic and distinctive buildings and structures.
- A variety of places of interest and activity.
- A variety of aesthetic and practical features, such as trees and street furniture.

# 7

# Accessibility

## WHY ACCESSIBILITY IS AN ESSENTIAL CHARACTERISTIC OF STREETS FOR LIFE

### WHAT DO WE MEAN BY ACCESSIBILITY?

Accessibility refers to the extent to which streets enable older people to reach, enter, use and walk around places they need or wish to visit, regardless of any physical, sensory or mental impairment. Accessible streets have local services and facilities, are connected to each other, have wide, flat footways and ground level signal-controlled pedestrian crossings.

### HOW ACCESSIBILITY AFFECTS OLDER USERS OF THE OUTDOOR ENVIRONMENT

#### Reaching their Destination

We have outlined in earlier chapters how features of the outdoor built environment are all too often designed with the average healthy young adult in mind. For example, the UK government states that 10 min is a comfortable walking time to reach services and facilities and calculates this is the time it takes to walk about 800 m (Department of Transport, Local Government and the Regions (DTLR), 2001). Llewelyn-Davies (2000) recommend that residential dwellings should have a post box and a telephone box located within 2–3 min (250 m) walking distance and a newsagent within 5 min (400 m) walking distance. They also

**Figure 7.1**   Older people generally cannot walk as far or as fast as younger adults.

suggest that local shops, a bus stop, a health centre and a place of worship should be situated within 10 min (800 m) walking distance. These calculations appear to be based on younger adults as people in their mid-70s will generally take around 10–20 min to walk 400 m to 500 m and cannot walk further than 10 min without a rest (American Institute of Architects (AIA), 1985; Carstens, 1985).

The majority of older people today will have been car drivers when they were younger but many eventually have to stop driving for safety or financial reasons at the very stage of life when walking and using public transport can be difficult and onerous. We found that 60 per cent of our participants without dementia and 75 per cent of the participants with dementia used a car when they were younger but that 40 per cent of those without dementia who drove and 100 per cent of those with dementia who drove have now given up driving. Greenberg (1982) found that older car users make around 25 per cent more journeys than older people without access to a car. This suggests that older people who do not drive do not stay at home through choice but because of the problems they encounter as pedestrians in the outdoor environment. As Greenberg explains:

> *age does not obviate the desire or necessity to go shopping, see the doctor, visit friends, and undertake other everyday activities – but it may alter the method and frequency with which they are done.* Greenberg (1982, p. 405)

Peace (1982) found that older people are more likely to use local facilities within walking distance of home, shop more often and make regular visits to medical facilities. As we outlined in Chapter 3, our research found similar patterns. Most of our research participants with dementia and all of those without dementia go out alone, over half in each group daily. All go shopping and around half also regularly visit the local post office, park or take walks around their local neighbourhood. Yet recent UK government research found that older people, especially those aged 75 years and over, experience far greater difficulties in accessing local services than younger people (Department of the Environment, Transport and the Regions (DETR) and Department of Health (DoH), 2001). This is hardly surprising if their design needs are not taken into consideration. Many of our participants are frail with reduced mobility or the unsteady gait often experienced by people with dementia. Those without dementia talked about places they have ceased to visit because they no longer feel able to cope with heavy traffic, crowded streets or a lack of essential public facilities, such as toilets and seating. They are also less likely to visit unfamiliar places than when they were younger due to the anxiety of not knowing their way around or where to find public facilities. Lavery *et al.* (1996, p. 183) note that, 'It is no exaggeration to say that the "average street" can be a very unfriendly place for older people' with many barriers, such as uneven or steep footways, poor lighting, inaccessible bus stops, or insufficient public toilets, seating or shelter. These unfriendly streets force older people experiencing temporary or permanent incapacity to either stay at home or to restrict their activities to local services and facilities, regardless of their quality or suitability (Peace, 1982).

Our participants with dementia are even more restricted in their independent use of the outdoor environment than other older people. As they are no longer able to drive or to use public transport on their own, they have to limit their independent trips to places within close walking distance of home. We talked in Chapter 5 about the anxiety carers experience when the person they care for fails to return home at the expected time. This often means that people with dementia are prevented by their carers from going out on their own because of the fear that they will become lost or involved in a traffic accident. All these problems make the accessibility and proximity of local services and facilities and the usability of streets and spaces essential factors in designing Streets for Life.

In the past, the movement of motorised traffic was often given priority when designing street layouts but, as Hillman (1990, p. 42) says, 'Roads go places, streets are places'. Planning policy now promotes the design of streets and neighbourhoods to help reduce car journeys by providing good quality local services and facilities and by making walking, cycling and using public transport pleasant and viable alternatives. Inclusive urban design recognises that successful neighbourhoods are those where the design of buildings, streets and spaces is based on the needs of all users at a human rather than vehicular scale. For people who are unable to drive this is a necessity which inclusive urban design seeks to achieve.

Older people living in relatively compact, mixed use areas with a combination of civic, commercial, leisure and residential properties should, in theory, find it easier to access facilities and services than those living in single use residential areas. As the Housing Corporation (2002) states: 'If neighbourhoods that include older people living in their own homes are to be sustainable, access to shops and services is essential'. However, the proximity of services and facilities is only one feature of accessibility. The quality and type of local services and facilities, the street layout and the quality of the design of the streets are also essential factors in Streets for Life.

## Walking along Unimpeded

We have already established that older people generally cannot walk as fast or as far as younger adults. A street layout with a number of dead-ends, such as culs-de-sac, is not only confusing in terms of legibility (see Chapter 5) but it also limits everyone's ability to move around on foot. Walking to local facilities in such neighbourhoods often means following a convoluted route that takes much longer than a direct connection would and pedestrian

**Figure 7.2** Crowded streets can be difficult to negotiate.

footpaths linking dead-ends typically run beyond back garden fences or rear access garage areas which are not overlooked and consequently feel isolated and unsafe.

For older people to be able to cope with crowded places they need enough space on the footway to walk along unimpeded without being jostled. However, as we outlined in Chapter 6, people with dementia tend to find it difficult to predict how other people will behave. This can be especially problematic in crowded places or on narrow footways where they are in danger of being jostled or knocked over because they are unable to anticipate which way an oncoming pedestrian may go.

Any level change can create barriers for people who are frail, have an unsteady gait or a visual impairment. People who find it difficult to lift their feet, such as those with arthritis, and people with visual impairments who struggle to see steps, find ramps easier to use. Other people, such as those with an unsteady balance, tend to find steps easier and safer than ramps, including a participant with dementia who said that 'ramps, especially zigzags, are very difficult to come down. They are tiring and unbalancing. Going down is harder than going up'. However, both steps and ramps can be challenging for people with mobility problems or low stamina; one participant with dementia explained that 'it depends on how tired I am and I appreciate the choice' while another told us that 'I would worry about tripping and falling but it's good to have a choice'. Steep changes are obviously particularly onerous but even slight level changes can be problematic as they are difficult to see and confusing to negotiate. All our participants without dementia and most of those with dementia complained that small steps can cause them

**Figure 7.3**   Below ground toilets are inaccessible to many people.

problems especially if they are not clearly marked, explaining that 'they are difficult to see' and 'you could easily trip up'.

The existence and accessibility of public toilets play an important role in enabling older people to spend time out of doors. Participants tend to avoid public toilets that are difficult to access, especially those below ground. The weight of doors to toilets, shops and facilities can also pose accessibility problems; for example, a participant without dementia complained that 'it's a problem to open the door and get in and then get out again before the door swings shut'. Consequently many participants plan their routes around department stores because, as a participant without dementia explained, 'shop toilets are cleaner, safer and have lifts to them' but these are less likely to be found in small local neighbourhoods than in town or city centres.

## HOW CAN ACCESSIBILITY BE ACHIEVED?

### ASPECTS AND FACTORS OF THE OUTDOOR ENVIRONMENT THAT HELP TO CREATE ACCESSIBILITY

### Local Facilities and Services

Older people should ideally live no further than 125 m from a telephone and post box, and no further than 500 m from essential services and facilities, including a general food store, post office, bank, general practitioner's (GP) surgery or health centre, green space (such as village green, green street edges), public toilets, seating and a bus stop. If secondary services and facilities, including a park or other form of open space, library, dentist, optician, places of worship, and community and leisure facilities, cannot also be within 500 m they should be no further than 800 m, again with public toilets and seating. The entrances to these services and facilities should be obvious and easy for older people to recognise. They should be at ground level wherever possible with flush thresholds. Public seating should ideally be positioned every 100 m to 125 m (for more information on seating please refer to Chapter 8).

### Street Layout

An accessible street layout is the same as a legible street layout (see Chapter 5). The streets are physically connected to each other, have clear views along them and simple junctions.

### Footways

Flat footways at least 2 m wide allow people with dementia, mobility problems and wheelchair users to safely pass oncoming pedestrians. A wide footway also

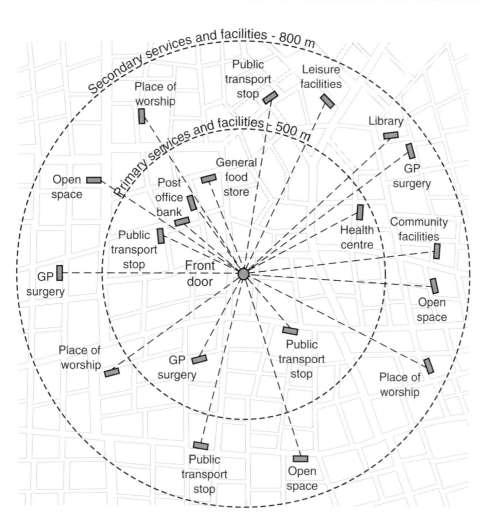

**Figure 7.4** Primary services and facilities should be within 500 m of older people's housing and secondary services should be within 800 m. (Drawing by Daniel Kozak.)

gives people a chance to walk a little further away from the motorised traffic travelling alongside on the road.

## Unavoidable Changes in Level

Accessible streets avoid changes in level wherever possible. However, where they are unavoidable, gentle slopes are easier for older people to see and negotiate than small steps. For greater inclines a ramp is necessary for people with wheelchairs, walking frames, pushchairs and shopping trolleys but to

**Figure 7.5** Wide footways provide more room for avoiding pedestrians and obstructions than narrow footways.

make a street accessible for older people both steps and a ramp should be provided.

There are a number of guides that detail the dimensions necessary for making ramps, steps and handrails accessible to older and disabled people. These include Oxley's *Inclusive Mobility* (2002), Carstens' *Site Planning and Design for the Elderly* (1985) and the AIA's *Design for Aging* (1985). In summary, however, ramps should have a maximum gradient of 1 in 20 or 5 per cent with level landings at the top and bottom. Steps should have clearly marked short straight runs with a minimum of three and a maximum of

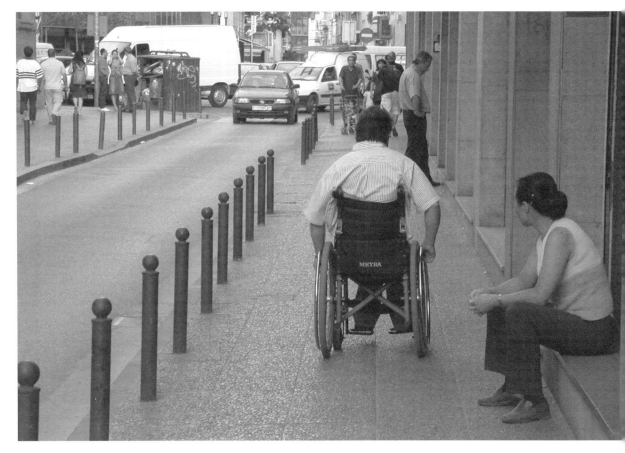

**Figure 7.6** Narrow footways impede accessibility.

twelve steps per run. Risers should be of uniform height (minimum 10 cm and maximum 15 cm high) and treads should be no shallower than 30 cm deep. Risers and treads should be in contrasting colours to help people with poor vision but patterns that are likely to cause dizziness should be avoided. Both ramps and steps should be clearly marked and well lit with guards and plain, non-slip, non-glare surfaces. Rounded handrails should always be provided on both sides in a smooth material that does not conduct heat or cold.

The design of pedestrian crossings is covered in Chapter 9 but the most important aspect for accessibility is that crossings should be at ground level rather than in the form of an underpass or footbridge. Public toilets should also be at ground level with doors that have no more than 2 kg pressure to open and levers that are easier to manipulate for people with weak or stiff hands than knobs.

**Figure 7.7**    Ideally, even small changes in level should have both a ramp and steps.

## DESIGN FEATURES AND CHARACTERISTICS OF ACCESSIBLE STREETS FOR LIFE

Accessible Streets for Life are likely to have:

- A mix of land uses.
- Housing located no further than 500 m from local primary services and facilities, including a general food store, post office, bank, GP surgery/health centre, green space (village green, green street edges), public toilets, public seating and public transport stops.
- Housing located no further than 800 m from local secondary services and facilities, including open space (parks, allotments, recreation grounds, public

squares), a library, dentist, optician, places of worship, community and leisure facilities and public toilets and seating.

- Obvious and easy to recognise entrances to places and buildings.
- Entrances at ground level whenever possible with flush thresholds.
- Public seating every 100 m to 125 m.
- Well connected streets with clear views along them and simple junctions.
- 2 m wide, flat footways.
- Gentle slopes rather than one or two small steps where slight level changes are unavoidable.
- A choice of steps and a ramp with a maximum gradient of 1 in 20 where greater level changes are unavoidable.
- Level changes (where unavoidable) that are clearly marked and well lit with guards, handrails and non-slip, non-glare surfaces.
- Pedestrian crossings and public toilets at ground level.
- Telephone boxes with level thresholds.
- Gates/doors with no more than 2 kg pressure to open and levers rather than knobs.

# 8

# Comfort

## WHY COMFORT IS AN ESSENTIAL CHARACTERISTIC OF STREETS FOR LIFE

### WHAT DO WE MEAN BY COMFORT?

Comfort refers to the extent to which streets enable people to visit places of their choice without physical or mental discomposure and to enjoy being out of the house. Comfortable streets are calm, welcoming and pedestrian-friendly with the services and facilities required by older people and people experiencing temporary or permanent incapacity.

### HOW DOES COMFORT AFFECT OLDER USERS OF THE OUTDOOR ENVIRONMENT?

#### Maintaining Independence

In Chapter 4 we outlined how many older people, especially those with dementia, find unfamiliar environments and features increasingly stressful to cope with and that they tend to restrict their activities to familiar local places as they grow older. The comfort of knowing where they are, where they can find the services and facilities they require and how local features work helps them to enjoy trips out of the house and to maintain their independence and self-esteem.

## Feeling Welcome

In Chapter 6 we discussed how the participants with dementia tend to prefer more informal, lively urban open spaces with plenty of features and activity that provide the necessary stimulation for those who need to maintain concentration. As well as their vitality, this type of open space also feels more welcoming; as a participant with dementia explained, 'it looks a friendly place and it has seats and I like the shops'. The term 'friendly' was also used to describe natural green open spaces, such as woodlands, which most of the participants favour over formal ones, such as botanical or historical gardens. The 'more human', welcoming nature of informal and natural open spaces provides a more psychologically comfortable environment for people who are aware of losing the ability to always understand what is expected of them in a particular environment, than formal places that can sometimes feel intimidating and forbidding.

## Enjoying Peace and Quiet

The fact that the participants choose to visit lively spaces does not mean that they feel comfortable in noisy or crowded places. A participant with dementia told us that, 'traffic is OK as long as I'm not too close to it as I don't like the noise and fumes'. In Chapter 5 we mentioned that sudden, loud noises often startle older people causing confusion and disorientation, especially for those with dementia. In addition, continuous noise, such as the drone of heavy traffic, affects their ability to hear. In fact, a participant without dementia told us that he has to turn his hearing aid off when he walks along heavily trafficked streets.

Although participants appreciate the interesting architecture of urban streets as much as the greener, leafier nature of suburban streets they can find urban traffic and crowds very difficult to cope with. A participant with dementia explained that, for her, 'towns are horrid to walk in because there are too many people blocking the pavement'. Given the choice, participants tend to avoid noisy, busy streets and find suburban and side streets more comfortable and pleasant to walk along.

Although the participants with dementia prefer lively, informal open spaces many, both with and without dementia, also referred to the positive benefits of open spaces being separated from motorised traffic and being able to sit quietly and watch the activity around them. This finding matches the recommendation of Llewelyn-Davies (2000, p. 99) that 'The best public spaces often have nodes of activity (with pavement cafes or markets, for example), complemented by quiet zones for rest and people-watching'.

## Meeting Physical Needs

In Chapter 5 we explained why short, gently winding streets are more legible than long, straight streets. They also feel more comfortable to walk along for people with reduced stamina, frailty or mobility problems as they 'feel less time-consuming even if it actually takes the same time'. Long, straight streets, on the other hand, are 'a bit overpowering', 'seem to go on interminably' and 'seem tedious even if they are not really'. On the accompanied walks participants rarely walked the whole length of long, straight streets unless there was no alternative.

Public seating, shelter and toilets are important factors in making a place or street comfortable, welcoming and easy to use for people of all ages and capabilities. A lack of these facilities was mentioned by a large number of participants as being a particular problem and a reason why they may not go out as often as they would like or why they avoid certain places.

For those who are willing or able to use public transport, seating and shelter at bus stops also helps to provide comfortable Streets for Life. Although open shelters are considered to be better than nothing, the majority of the

**Figure 8.1** The wooden seat with back and arm rests provides a far more comfortable resting place than the metal bench. Litter bins should have swing lids to protect against odours and wasps and be emptied regularly!

participants prefer enclosed shelters with transparent walls or large clear windows, which protect them from the wind and rain while enabling them to see buses coming. The transparency also makes them feel safer as they can see who is in the shelter when they arrive and they can be seen by passers-by while they are waiting. A number of participants referred to the difficulty of using the seats in many bus shelters as they are too small, are made of a hard, smooth material and often tilt downwards; for example, a participant without dementia complained that 'they are very shiny and you cannot sit on them, well I can't, without hanging on to something'.

In Chapter 4 we explained the popularity of the traditional red K6 telephone box due to older people being familiar with its appearance and function. Whether traditional or modern, enclosed telephone boxes are also felt to be more comfortable to use than open kiosks as they provide privacy and

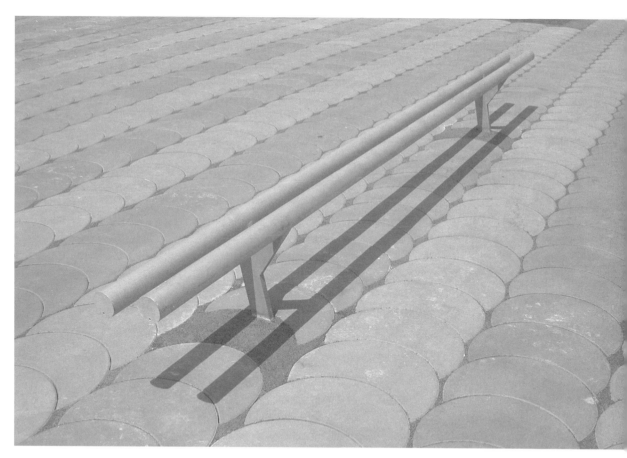

**Figure 8.2** This bench could not be more un-friendly if it tried! It does not look familiar, comfortable or even safe and is situated on paving guaranteed to cause dizziness.

protection from noise and weather. As a participant with dementia exclaimed when shown a photograph of an open kiosk, 'I and the phones would get wet!'

Many older people cannot walk for longer than 10 min without resting and although our participants are grateful to have anywhere to sit down when they need to, some styles and materials are far more user-friendly and comfortable for older people than others. Participants prefer to use seats with both back and arm rests. The back rest gives comfortable support and the arm rests provide something to hold onto when sitting down and to push down on when standing up. Low seats and benches without back or arm rests are considered very uncomfortable and difficult to use. Wooden seats are also the most popular as they feel warmer and more comfortable than those made of metal or concrete which, as a participant with dementia declared, 'look slippery and hard and uncomfortable and not good taste'. Wooden seats are also considered to be more familiar, attractive and welcoming than the more modern types made of hard materials. As a participant without dementia said of the latter, 'they may be vandal proof but they look horrendous'. Some of the more modern obscure styles of bench, such as the one illustrated in Figure 8.2 are also difficult for older people with dementia to recognise as seating at all!

In Chapter 2 we explained that older people tend to need to visit the toilet more often than when they were younger. Most of our participants reminisced about a time when public toilets were easy to find and safe and pleasant to use due to the presence of an attendant. As we mentioned in Chapter 7, the lack of public toilets prevents some older people from going out as often as they would like. We have also already explained that our participants with dementia struggle to understand modern designs that are unfamiliar to them while those without dementia often fear that they will not be able to understand or cope with the new technology. This is the case with the automated 'Superloo' public convenience capsules that many local authorities are now installing. These are either not recognised as being public toilets or are treated with suspicion by most of our participants who fear that they will not understand how to use them or that they may become trapped inside. One participant thought they looked 'terribly forbidding' while another was more willing to give them the benefit of the doubt with the observation that 'it looks nasty and modern but it may be more comfortable to use'.

# HOW CAN COMFORT BE ACHIEVED?

## ASPECTS AND FACTORS OF THE OUTDOOR ENVIRONMENT THAT HELP TO CREATE COMFORT

### The Comfort of Familiarity

For older people, a comfortable street is also generally a familiar one with buildings and features in designs they recognise and understand (see Chapter 4).

### Welcoming Open Spaces

Open spaces should be small enough so that they are not daunting for older people to enter and well defined with the use of low fencing, walls or hedges. Active areas, such as ponds, playgrounds and cafes, help to make older people with dementia feel welcome and that it is all right for them to be there. They are also more likely to attract other users so that the open space does not feel isolated or threatening. However, they should also have places away from, but not out of sight of, busy areas where people can sit and enjoy some tranquillity away from crowds and traffic. Seating and lighting in open spaces are essential. Shelter and public toilets should at least be within walking distance of the open space.

### Quiet Streets

The hierarchy of streets recommended earlier to promote familiarity and legibility also gives people the choice of walking along quiet side roads as alternative routes away from the crowds and traffic generally found on larger, main streets. Making some streets pedestrianised with seating and shelter provides another opportunity for people to escape the traffic. Acoustic barriers and buffers, such as fencing, trees and shrubs, help to shield pedestrians from traffic and to reduce street and background noises.

### Undaunting Streets

Comfortable streets are the same as legible streets (see Chapter 5). They are relatively short and gently winding so that they do not give the impression of being tedious and interminable. They are also connected to each other so that people can take direct routes to their destinations.

### Bus Stops

Wherever possible, bus stops should have some form of shelter, preferably enclosed with transparent sides or large clear windows. Shelters should have wide, flat seats made of non-slippery materials that do not conduct heat or cold.

**Figure 8.3**  The automated 'Superloo' is unfamiliar and a little daunting to many older people who will seek out more conventional types of public toilet.

## Telephone Boxes

As we mentioned earlier, many of the participants without dementia appreciate the accessibility of modern telephone boxes but still generally regard them as unattractive. Incorporating the familiarity and distinctiveness of the

**Figure 8.4**   A conventional type of public toilet. (Photograph by SURFACE Inclusive Design Research Centre.)

traditional red K6 telephone box with the easier to use features, such as level thresholds and lighter doors, of the modern boxes would provide comfortable enclosed telephone boxes for everyone to use that people with dementia would also recognise and continue to be able to use as wayfinding cues.

## Public Seating

Many local authorities seem more interested in preventing vandalism than providing seating that is attractive, comfortable and easy to use. Seats that are easy and comfortable for older people to use are sturdy with continuous back rests, protruding arm rests and non-protruding legs. They are made of

**Figure 8.5**    Open spaces should have quiet, shaded seating areas.

wood or other soft materials that do not conduct heat or cold. We mentioned that a number of participants complained that some public seating is too low. According to Oxley (2002), guidance on seating heights varies from 420 mm to 580 mm. Carstens (1985) notes that 90 per cent of people over the age of 75 years are less than 164 cm in height and recommends that seating should

**Figure 8.6**   Older people prefer enclosed bus shelters with seating and transparent sides or large windows. (Photograph by SURFACE Inclusive Design Research Centre.)

be no more than 440 mm high. Oxley (2002), however, also makes the useful observation that seats of different heights are used by some providers to cater for both short and tall people. We would, therefore, recommend providing seats at both 420 mm to 440 mm and 470 mm to 480 mm heights.

Seating should be every 100 m to 125 m. Where possible, for example in open spaces, positioning some seating at right-angles to each other allows people with poor hearing or eyesight to see and chat to their companions.

**Public Toilets**

The most comfortable public conveniences for older people are ground level conventional toilets situated in view of passers-by and neighbouring buildings.

## DESIGN FEATURES AND CHARACTERISTICS OF COMFORTABLE STREETS FOR LIFE

Comfortable Streets for Life are likely to have:

- A calm, welcoming feel
- Familiar buildings and features in designs older people recognise
- Small, quiet well-defined open spaces, free from motorised traffic and with seating, lighting, toilets and shelter
- Quiet side roads as alternative routes away from crowds and traffic
- Some pedestrianised areas to offer protection from traffic
- Acoustic barriers, such as planting and fencing, to reduce background noise
- Relatively short, gently winding and well-connected streets
- Enclosed bus shelters with seating and transparent walls or large clear windows
- Enclosed telephone boxes
- Sturdy public seating every 100 m to 125 m with arm and back rests and in materials that do not conduct heat or cold
- Ground level conventional public toilets in view of buildings and pedestrians.

# Safety

## WHY SAFETY IS AN ESSENTIAL CHARACTERISTIC OF STREETS FOR LIFE

### WHAT DO WE MEAN BY SAFETY?

Safety refers to the extent to which streets enable people to use, enjoy and move around the outside environment without fear of tripping or falling, being run-over or being attacked. Safe streets have buildings facing onto them, separate bicycle lanes and wide, well-lit, plain, smooth footways.

### HOW SAFETY AFFECTS OLDER USERS OF THE OUTDOOR ENVIRONMENT

In Chapter 3 we described how the participants with dementia were far less likely to talk about problems that they face when they are outside than those without dementia. The few who did mention problems focused on how their own physical impairments, such as poor eyesight or an unsteady gait, cause them to stumble and fall when they go outside. Those without dementia discussed a variety of physical issues relating to the safety of their local neighbourhoods including uneven paving and bicycles on footways. They also

**Figure 9.1**    Bicycles on footways are a common safety concern for older people.

talked about psychological difficulties, such as the fear of falling or of being attacked. However, findings from the accompanied walks confirm that people with dementia experience similar problems to those described by the participants without dementia but appear to be less aware of them. Furthermore, those who lost their way during the accompanied walks were far less aware of potential problems, obstacles and dangers, such as uneven paving or broken street furniture, than those, with and without dementia, who did not lose their way. This means that hazards that are potentially dangerous to any user pose even more of a threat to people who are confused and/or experiencing memory or orientation problems.

**Figure 9.2**   Older people find broken or uneven parking particularly hazardous.

## Fear of Being Attacked

As mentioned above, many of the participants without dementia worry about being attacked while they are out and the majority do not go out alone after dark because of this. One participant told us that she feels 'frightened of walking in empty places', another that he does not like empty streets or places because they 'look very very lonely and you're all on your own if anything happens'. A third told us she avoids streets or alleyways that are not overlooked because she 'would worry about being attacked as no one would see or hear'. They also avoid places where 'you can't see what's down there', such as toilets below ground and underpasses where 'you get these kids rushing around and you never quite know who you're going to meet round the corner'. However, quiet alleyways or footpaths are not so daunting if they are a short, direct connection between two busy streets where both ends are visible. If they are also overlooked by doors and windows they feel even less threatening.

In Chapter 8 we outlined how the participants generally prefer enclosed telephone boxes because of the protection they give from the weather and from noise. Open telephone kiosks are not only considered uncomfortable to use but also potentially dangerous because the user's back is exposed to passers-by making him/her feel vulnerable and anxious. For example, one participant without dementia said that she would be concerned that 'people could see your purse' and another told us she would worry that 'people could attack you'.

### Fear of Being Run-over

Many participants are anxious about being knocked over by cyclists on the footway, whether or not there is a delineated cycle track on the footway. A participant with dementia explained that the problem for him is that 'it's difficult to remember which side to walk on and I've got enough to think about making sure I don't get lost.' Those without dementia are more concerned that the cyclists do not stay in their designated lane or that they come up so quietly behind them at speed that the shock of them suddenly rushing past unbalances and upsets them. A further safety problem is vehicles parked on or half way on the footway so that pedestrians not only have little room to pass-by but are also at risk from maneuvering vehicles.

Wide roads are generally unpopular with our participants. Comments included 'they look very fast' and 'they are too easy for cars to speed on'. They are also viewed as more dangerous to cross, particularly when there are no pedestrian crossings. Crossing a wide or busy road can be a difficult task for anybody but for people with slow reactions, reduced cognitive abilities or mobility problems it can be dangerous and stressful even at controlled crossings as a participant with dementia demonstrated on his accompanied walk, 'Well, we'll have to cross the road but we'll wait a moment. I think if we cross here and then . . . oh, we'll cross now, it's quiet . . . no, it's not! It'll be green in a moment, be green in a moment. It does well to wait. We can't run like we used to'.

We expected the participants to list Zebra crossings (black and white strips across the road with an orange flashing beacon on both sides of the street but no traffic signals) as their preferred road crossing because they have been in existence for such a long time. However, we found that most of the participants, with and without dementia, do not trust drivers to stop at them or to wait long enough for them to safely reach the other side. A participant without dementia explained how at Zebra crossings she feels it is necessary to 'get my husband to put his stick out but cars still don't always stop'.

**Figure 9.3**   Cars parked half on footways are dangerous and obstructive.

The Pelican crossing (Pedestrian Light-Controlled Crossing), which is one of three types of signal-controlled crossing in the UK, is the most popular type of crossing with the participants who consider them to be 'the safest for older people'. They have been in existence long enough to be familiar and participants feel confident that vehicles will stop when the traffic light turns red. However, a problem with some signal-controlled crossings is that older people often have difficulty hearing higher frequency sounds. Another problem is that it takes older people longer to react than younger adults once they have realised that it is safe to cross and longer to cross the road; as a participant without dementia commented, 'they are a good idea but they don't give enough time to cross especially for slow older people'. Toucan crossings, which are signal-controlled crossings shared by pedestrians and cyclists, are unpopular due to the problems mentioned above about sharing footways with cyclists. Although Puffin crossings (Pedestrian User-Friendly Intelligent Crossing), which automatically give each pedestrian the time s/he needs to cross the road, have been in existence for around 10 years our participants expressed astonishment when asked about them and insisted that they had never heard of them. For people with dementia this could be attributed to their memory problems but for those without dementia we can only assume that not enough public information has been provided about them. At first glance, Pelican and Puffin crossings look very similar but the former have a visual signal on both the near and far sides of the road whereas the Puffin crossing only displays a visual signal next to the push button. Neither does the Puffin crossing give the flashing amber and green man periods that older people are used to seeing at Pelican crossings. If people presume that they are at Pelican crossings the failure of the Puffin crossing to act in the way that they expect could cause confusion and therefore be potentially dangerous.

Non-controlled traffic islands are considered very useful for less busy wide roads by most of the participants as they enable them to cross the road in two stages and to pause for a rest or a break in the traffic in the middle. Under-passes and foot bridges are generally avoided because 'it's such a long way to walk' and the effort required to go up and down the steep slopes or steps is too onerous for them.

## Fear of Falling

We mentioned in Chapter 2 that about one third of people aged 65 years and over and around half of those aged 85 years and over will fall at least once a year. Research has found that after they have fallen some older people will either not go out as often as before or will not go out alone due to the fear of falling again (Campbell, 2005). In Chapter 7 we explained that people with dementia also cannot always interpret the intentions of oncoming pedestrians. This increases the risk of being jostled or knocked over as by the time they realise they are in someone's path they do not have the agility to move out of the way. This will also be the case for many people with visual or mobility impairments. People with dementia often walk with a slow, unsteady shuffling gait so that coarse textured paving materials, such as cobbles, and paving that is uneven or has dislodged paving slabs or manhole covers are particularly difficult for them to walk along without tripping or stumbling. The tactile

**Figure 9.4**   Underpasses can be onerous and frightening.

paving used at dropped kerbs for people with visual impairments is generally not understood by the participants with dementia and while those without dementia tend to accept the reasons for their use they consider them to be a trip hazard and uncomfortable to walk on, especially when badly maintained. It was also pointed out to us that the edges of larger slabs are easier to see by people with visual impairments that small-block paving so that if they are uneven there is a better chance of noticing and negotiating them. However, flat, smooth paving, such as those made of tarmac, are felt to be the safest to walk on if not the most attractive. We found that a number of our participants always make sure that they wear walking boots or flat, study shoes when they go outside due to the poor quality of the paving in their neighbourhoods.

As we also mentioned in Chapter 2, people with diminished visual acuity often mistake sharp colour contrasts or paving patterns for steps or holes. Busy patterns, such as chessboard squares or repetitive lines can also cause dizziness and shiny or reflective surfaces are seen as wet and slippery. Trying to negotiate these patterns can cause people to stumble or become disoriented. When shown a photograph of a geometric-paving pattern using pale yellow paving slabs and dark brown block paving many participants thought walking along such paving might make them dizzy and that the lines could be confused as steps. A participant with dementia also told us that 'I would be tempted to walk along the brown lines and run round the pattern'. A participant without dementia made the interesting observation that 'my epileptic sister might be a bit risky with this one'. A picture of small dark grey block paving laid out in a repetitive circular pattern was considered more attractive by most of the participants than the two-tone geometric pattern but still a cause for concern. A participant with dementia told us that 'it would be all right in small quantities but if there is too much I might feel giddy and going round in circles. A friend has them in her drive and it makes me giddy as there is so much of it'. A number of participants also mentioned that they would find it difficult to walk on the rough surface created by the small blocks.

Older people often trip going up or down steps and curbs as they cannot clearly see the edge. People with poor visual acuity also have an increased sensitivity to glare and find it difficult to focus when moving between dark shadow and bright light. This can cause people to lose their balance, or to become disoriented or confused (American Institute of Architects (AIA), 1985). Again, the patterns on the ground made by extremes of dark shadow and bright light can appear to be level changes to people with visual impairments.

Streets devoid of clutter are also easier and safer for people with mobility, visual or concentration problems to walk along. Many participants mentioned the hazards of negotiating street clutter as they walk along and both participants with and without dementia talked about how difficult it can be to walk down a street full of signs, bollards, poles, litterbins, grit-bins, bicycle racks and railings. 'Dreadful', 'a nightmare' and 'appalling' were some of the adjectives used to describe cluttered streets.

**Figure 9.5** These cobbled strips are a trip hazard – not only are they slightly raised but they will look like steps to people with impaired depth perception.

**Figure 9.6**  The rough surface of this paving can be difficult for older people and others with mobility problems to walk on. The pattern is likely to cause dizziness and confusion in people with visual and cognitive impairments.

# HOW CAN SAFETY BE ACHIEVED?

## ASPECTS AND FACTORS OF THE OUTDOOR ENVIRONMENT THAT HELP TO CREATE SAFETY

### Natural Surveillance

In Chapter 7 we referred to the fact that older people living in mixed use neighbourhoods are generally more able to access the services and facilities they need than those living in solely residential areas. Neighbourhoods that provide a mix of uses relevant to the needs of local people will also be active places that help older people to feel less vulnerable, providing they are not overcrowded.

In Chapter 4 we discussed the need for buildings, doors and windows to face the street to present a more familiar environment for older people and to help people with dementia to identify what the buildings are for. In Chapter 5 we also explained that buildings facing the street help to provide a visually interesting street frontage and a clear distinction between public and private space. They also help to make people walking along the street feel safer because it is reassuring to feel that the street can be seen by the occupants of the buildings.

Segregated pedestrian routes, such as alleyways and snickets, can be a useful means of connecting other routes and, if designed well, can also provide attractive and interesting paths for people to explore and enjoy. However, if they are lined by blank walls or fencing or go through places that are seldom used people will feel vulnerable and unwilling to use them. Segregated pedestrian routes should be very short, should connect to busier streets and be overlooked by windows and doors.

In Chapter 5 we explained how the irregular grid pattern with corners greater than 90° and gently winding streets where the vista slowly opens up as one walks along provides an interesting and legible street layout for older people. It also helps people to feels safer than a street with blind bends where one cannot tell what might be around the corner.

### Pedestrian Crossings

Wherever possible, but particularly on busier and wider roads, ground level signal-controlled pedestrian crossings should be provided. Audible signals should be at a fairly low pitch so that people with hearing impairments can hear them and there should also always be a visual signal. Although the Pelican crossing has a fixed time limit set to the demands of the particular road it is on, it is more familiar to older people than the Puffin crossing and has a visual signal on both sides of the road which is not only more familiar to older people but enables people to reassure themselves that it is safe to cross as they make their way across the road. Combining the familiarity of the Pelican design with

**Figure 9.7**   Older people feel safer using signal-controlled pedestrian crossings with audible cues and visual signals on both sides of the road than other types of crossing. (Photograph by SURFACE Inclusive Design Research Centre.)

the Puffin's ability to detect when a person is still on the crossing would be ideal. Traffic islands are a good alternative for roads where traffic levels are lower than on main roads.

It is essential to ensure that speed humps and entry treatments do not resemble pedestrian crossings in any way. Those surfaced with black tarmac with white arrows painted on them to show the direction of traffic look dangerously similar to Zebra crossings.

## Footways

In Chapter 7 we recommend that footways should be at least 2 m wide to allow people with dementia or mobility problems and wheelchair users to safely pass

**Figure 9.8**  Footways should be wide with plain, smooth, level, non-slip and non-reflective paving.

oncoming pedestrians. A wide footway also gives people a chance to walk a little further away from the motorised traffic moving alongside on the road.

Footways should not be split between pedestrians and cyclists. In Chapter 8 we suggest using trees to buffer pedestrians on the footway from the noise of the traffic. A line of trees and a grass verge between the footway and road also helps to delineate the footway from the road and discourages or prevents drivers from parking their vehicles on the footway. As wet leaves can be slippery under foot it is better to use evergreens or trees with small leaves that disperse in the wind.

On-street parking can also provide an extra barrier between pedestrians and traffic and helps to slow the traffic down. A line of parked cars is not, of course, as attractive as grass and trees but parking spaces can be interspersed with some trees or planting.

The safest paving for older people to walk on is plain, smooth, level, non-slip and non-reflective. Tarmac is the safest paving material for older people to walk on followed by large paving slabs providing they are flat and smooth. Grates and drains should be flush with paving with openings smaller than walking stick or shoe heel size. Although paving patterns should be avoided on footways a distinctive change in paving colour or material can be useful for discouraging people from stepping onto hazardous areas such as bicycle lanes. Walls should be in contrasting colours and materials to paving so that people with visual problems can see them more clearly.

Buildings should be designed and oriented to avoid creating areas of extreme dark and light on the footway. Footways should also be clear of any unnecessary street clutter.

## DESIGN FEATURES AND CHARACTERISTICS OF SAFE STREETS FOR LIFE

Safe Streets for Life are likely to have:

- A mix of uses
- Buildings, doors and windows facing the street
- Clearly marked bicycle lanes separate from footways
- Pedestrians separated from traffic by trees, on-road parking or bicycle lanes
- Signal-controlled pedestrian crossings with visual signals on both sides of the crossing and audible cues at a pitch and timing suitable for frail older people
- Traffic calming measures in clear colour and textural contrast to footways and pedestrian crossings
- Wide, well-maintained, clean footways
- Plain, non-reflective paving in clear colour and textural contrast to walls, bicycle lanes and traffic calming measures
- Flat, smooth, non-slip paving
- Grates and drains flush with paving with openings smaller than walking stick or shoe heel size
- Trees with narrow leaves that do not stick to paving when wet
- Spaces and buildings designed and oriented to avoid areas of dark shadow or bright light
- Street lighting adequate for people with visual impairments
- Some enclosed telephone boxes.

# PART III

# Streets for Life:
# The Future?

# CHAPTER 10

# Streets for Life
# in practice

## INTRODUCTION

The previous six chapters, making up Part 2 of the book, outlined the design guidelines stemming from our dementia research. We believe that these guidelines, if put into practice, will contribute towards creating Streets for Life. We have 65 recommendations, within the six categories of familiarity, legibility, distinctiveness, accessibility, comfort and safety.

The aim of this chapter is to explain how the principles and recommendations outlined in Part 2 can be put into practice, and to highlight other issues and objectives that need to be considered. The sections below will discuss: when and where the recommendations could be used; the people who, through their work and activities, might be responsible for using them; and the approaches and principles they should have in doing so.

## WHEN AND WHERE?

We developed the Streets for Life recommendations to be of use in a wide variety of situations. Obviously, the ideal situation for creating Streets for Life is when designing whole new towns and settlements. With the initiation of the Sustainable Communities Plan by the UK government (Office of the Deputy Prime Minister (ODPM), 2003), such new development may well be delivered, and using these Streets for Life recommendations will contribute to sustainability. However, we realise that in the overall scheme of things, these new communities are relatively uncommon; urban areas tend to be modified slowly over time, and the rate of change of the built environment is very small. So we need recommendations that can also be used when redeveloping or regenerating urban areas. Some of the recommendations can only be implemented in new development, but there are many that are valid for existing areas, as outlined below.

## CREATING NEW URBAN AREAS

We have picked out seventeen recommendations to form the key design features of Streets for Life:

1. Small blocks laid out on an irregular grid (with minimal crossroads).
2. A hierarchy of streets from main to side.
3. Gently winding streets.
4. Varied urban form and architecture.
5. A mix of uses, including plenty of services and facilities and open space.
6. Busy routes with buffer zone between road and footway (e.g. trees, grass verge).
7. Buildings designed to reflect uses.
8. Buildings with obvious entrances.
9. Landmarks, distinctive structures and places of activity.
10. Special/distinctive features at junctions.
11. Wide, smooth, non-slip footways (without cycle lanes).
12. Frequent road crossings with audible and visual cues suitable for older people.
13. Clearly marked level changes, with handrails.
14. Clear signs throughout.
15. Frequent wooden seating, with arm and back rests.
16. Enclosed bus shelters, with seating.
17. Ground level toilets.

These are illustrated in Figure 10.1. We consider this to be the most important diagram in the book – it summarises the essential ingredients of our dementia-friendly approach.

These recommendations can be used when designing:

- New towns
- New urban extensions
- New 'urban villages' on existing urban or suburban land

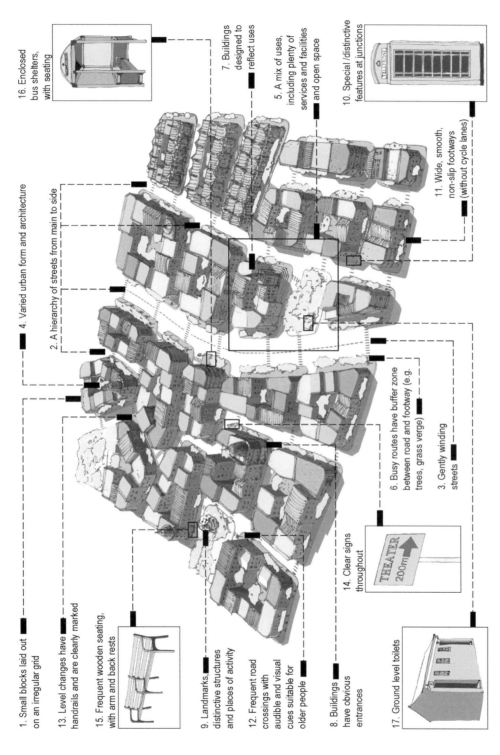

16. Enclosed bus shelters, with seating

7. Buildings designed to reflect uses

5. A mix of uses, including plenty of services and facilities and open space

10. Special/distinctive features at junctions

4. Varied urban form and architecture

2. A hierarchy of streets from main to side

11. Wide, smooth, non-slip footways (without cycle lanes)

6. Busy routes have buffer zone between road and footway (e.g. trees, grass verge)

3. Gently winding streets

1. Small blocks laid out on an irregular grid

13. Level changes have handrails and are clearly marked

15. Frequent wooden seating, with arm and back rests

9. Landmarks, distinctive structures and places of activity

12. Frequent road crossings with audible and visual cues suitable for older people

8. Buildings have obvious entrances

14. Clear signs throughout

17. Ground level toilets

**Figure 10.1**   The key design features of Streets for Life. (Drawing by Daniel Kozak.)

133

- Sustainable communities
- Large housing developments, private or social.

We suggest the recommendations are considered as early in the design process as possible. Some can only be implemented at this stage (e.g. those related to overall urban layout and street network/shape). Others need to be considered at the detailed design stage (e.g. footway/road design), while others, including those to do with street furniture, can be implemented near the end of the design process.

## ADAPTING EXISTING URBAN AREAS

The Streets for Life recommendations can be used when adapting existing urban areas, in a number of different situations:

- Re-development of urban areas
- Regeneration of run-down areas
- Infill development
- Small-scale additions/new buildings
- Small-scale changes to open spaces
- Refurbishment/replacement of street furniture.

The key recommendations that should be considered when adapting existing urban areas are:

1. Ensure changes are small-scale and incremental.
2. Increase, where possible, the number of pedestrian and vehicular connections between streets, to reduce block sizes (e.g. create new streets or passageways).
3. Increase the mix in uses through new buildings and facilities.
4. Add landmarks, distinctive structures, open spaces or places of activity.
5. Make sure new buildings contribute to local character and variety (through detail including colours, windows, roof tiling, as well as overall form).
6. Add special features (e.g. post boxes, telephone boxes, trees, statues) at junctions, particularly complex ones.
7. Add porches, canopies and clear signs to make entrances to public buildings obvious.
8. Increase the widths of footways (e.g. by reducing the widths of roads).
9. On busy roads, create a buffer zone between pedestrians and cars (e.g. through trees, grass verges).
10. Move cycle lanes from footways to roads.
11. Increase the frequency of pedestrian crossings.
12. Where there are steps, attempt to provide a slope or ramp (no more than 1 in 20) as well.
13. Add handrails to steps or ramps, if they do not have them.

14. Fix clear signs and symbols (where existing ones are poor) to publicly accessible buildings, preferably perpendicular to walls.
15. Remove all unclear and unnecessary signs.
16. Replace all unclear road and directional signs with clear ones (i.e. those with large graphics and realistic symbols in clear contrast to the background, preferably dark lettering on a light background) – all directional signs should be single pointers.
17. Increase variety in the existing built form (e.g. by painting doors and windows different colours and adding details such as window boxes).
18. Only use seats, telephone boxes, bus shelters and toilets that are suitable for older people (see individual recommendations for details).
19. Replace gates and doors where necessary so they require no more than 2 kg of pressure to open and have lever handles.
20. Improve audible and visual cues at pedestrian crossings and increase crossing time where necessary.
21. Replace cobbled, rough or patterned footways with smooth, plain ones.
22. Reduce street clutter (e.g. boards, adverts, signs).
23. Increase the amount of street lighting where necessary.

Or, where no development or major change is planned, some of the recommendations could still be implemented in urban areas to bring them closer to Streets for Life and make them more sustainable. For example:

1. Add landmarks, distinctive structures, open spaces or places of activity.
2. Add special features (e.g. post boxes, telephone boxes, trees, statues) at junctions, particularly complex ones.
3. Add porches, canopies and clear signs to make entrances to public buildings obvious.
4. Increase the widths of footways (e.g. by reducing the widths of roads).
5. On busy roads, create a buffer zone between pedestrians and cars (e.g. through trees, grass verges).
6. Move cycle lanes from footways to roads.
7. Increase the frequency of pedestrian crossings.
8. Where there are steps, attempt to provide a slope or ramp (no more than 1 in 20) as well.
9. Add handrails to steps or ramps, if they do not have them.
10. Fix clear signs and symbols (where existing ones are poor) to publicly accessible buildings, preferably perpendicular to walls.
11. Remove all unclear and unnecessary signs.
12. Replace all unclear road and directional signs with clear ones (i.e. those with large graphics and realistic symbols in clear contrast to the background, preferably dark lettering on a light background) – all directional signs should be single pointers.
13. Increase variety in the existing built form (e.g. by painting doors and windows different colours and adding details such as window boxes).

14. Only use seats, telephone boxes, bus shelters and toilets that are suitable for older people (see individual recommendations for details).
15. Replace gates and doors where necessary so they require no more than 2 kg of pressure to open and have lever handles.
16. Improve audible and visual cues at pedestrian crossings and increase crossing time where necessary.
17. Replace cobbled, rough or patterned footways with smooth, plain ones
18. Reduce street clutter (e.g. boards, adverts, signs).
19. Increase the amount of street lighting where necessary.

Regular maintenance of streets in itself makes a positive contribution to creating Streets for Life. The research participants frequently mentioned lack of maintenance as one of the biggest problems they face when going outdoors. They were particularly concerned about broken paving and potholes, which caused them to trip or stumble. They also worried about slipping on leaves in the autumn and winter, if they were not regularly swept up, and wanted hedges and trees lining footways to be regularly cut back and trimmed.

## WHO?

There are a number of professions, organisations and groups that could be involved in implementing our Streets for Life recommendations. Most of these are practitioners engaged in producing or maintaining outdoor areas, but there are also policy makers who could help to make Streets for Life a reality.

In terms of policy, we would like to see the Streets for Life concept adopted and promoted in land-use planning policy, housing policy and urban policy. The concept could also form part of policies on sustainable development (i.e. the social aspects). The specific recommendations may be contained in supplementary guidance for any of these policies. They are already being promoted by the Housing Corporation for new affordable housing schemes, through the leaflet, *Neighbourhoods for Life: A Checklist of Recommendations for Designing Dementia-Friendly Outdoor Environments* (Mitchell, Burton and Raman, 2004).

In terms of practice, we are aiming the recommendations at the following people:

- Producers of street environments:
    - Architects
    - Urban designers
    - Planners
    - Highways engineers
    - Private developers
    - Housing associations
    - Manufacturers of street furniture.

**Neighbourhoods for Life**

A checklist of recommendations for designing dementia-friendly outdoor environments

**Figure 10.2** Recommendations leaflet for housing associations, sponsored by the Housing Corporation (Mitchell, Burton and Raman 2004).

- Managers/maintainers of street environments:
    - Local authority maintenance departments
    - Local authority planning and highways departments
    - Access officers
    - Town centre managers
    - Shopping centre and other property managers
    - Local residents.

Obviously the different groups of people will have control or influence over different sets of recommendations, as summarised in Table 10.1.

**Table 10.1** Streets for Life recommendations for different implementing bodies.

| Recommendation | Implementing body | | | | | | | | | | | |
|---|---|---|---|---|---|---|---|---|---|---|---|---|
| | Architects | Urban designers | Planners (development control) | Highway engineers | Private developers | Not-for-profit developers | Street furniture manufacturers | Maintenance departments | Access officers | Town centre managers | Property managers | Local residents |
| **Creating new urban areas** | | | | | | | | | | | | |
| 1. Small blocks laid out on an irregular grid (with minimal cross-roads) | ✓ | ✓ | ✓ | ✓ | ✓ | ✓ | | | | | | |
| 2. A hierarchy of streets from main to side | ✓ | ✓ | ✓ | ✓ | ✓ | ✓ | | | | | | |
| 3. Gently winding streets | ✓ | ✓ | ✓ | ✓ | ✓ | ✓ | | | | | | |
| 4. Varied urban form and architecture | ✓ | ✓ | ✓ | | ✓ | ✓ | | | | | | |
| 5. A mix of uses, including plenty of services and facilities and open space | ✓ | ✓ | ✓ | | ✓ | ✓ | | | | | | |
| 6. Busy routes with buffer zone between road and footway (e.g. trees, grass verge) | ✓ | ✓ | ✓ | ✓ | ✓ | | | | | | | |

| | C1 | C2 | C3 | C4 | C5 | C6 | C7 | C8 |
|---|---|---|---|---|---|---|---|---|
| 7. Buildings designed to reflect uses | ✓ | ✓ | | | | ✓ | | |
| 8. Buildings with obvious entrances | ✓ | ✓ | | | | ✓ | | |
| 9. Landmarks, distinctive structures and places of activity | ✓ | ✓ | | | | ✓ | | |
| 10. Special/distinctive features at junctions | ✓ | ✓ | ✓ | | | ✓ | | |
| 11. Wide, smooth, non-slip footways (without cycle lanes) | ✓ | ✓ | ✓ | | ✓ | ✓ | | |
| 12. Frequent road crossings with audible cues suitable for older people | ✓ | ✓ | ✓ | | ✓ | ✓ | | |
| 13. Clearly marked level changes, with handrails | ✓ | ✓ | ✓ | | ✓ | ✓ | | |
| 14. Clear signs throughout | ✓ | ✓ | | ✓ | ✓ | ✓ | ✓ | |
| 15. Frequent wooden seating, with arm and back rests | | ✓ | | ✓ | ✓ | ✓ | ✓ | |
| 16. Enclosed bus shelters, with seating | | | | ✓ | | | ✓ | |
| 17. Ground level toilets | ✓ | ✓ | | ✓ | | ✓ | ✓ | ✓ |

(Continued)

139

**Table 10.1** [*Continued*].

### Adapting existing urban areas

| | Architects | Urban designers | Planners (development control) | Highway engineers | Private developers | Not-for-profit developers | Street furniture manufacturers | Maintenance departments | Access officers | Town centre managers | Property managers | Local residents |
|---|---|---|---|---|---|---|---|---|---|---|---|---|
| 1. Ensure changes are small-scale and incremental | ✓ | ✓ | ✓ | | ✓ | ✓ | | | | | | |
| 2. Increase, where possible, the number of pedestrian and vehicular connections between streets, to reduce block sizes (e.g. create new streets or passageways) | ✓ | ✓ | ✓ | ✓ | ✓ | ✓ | | | | ✓ | | |
| 3. Increase the mix in uses through new buildings and facilities | ✓ | ✓ | ✓ | | ✓ | ✓ | | | | ✓ | | |
| 4. Add landmarks, distinctive structures, open spaces or places of activity | ✓ | ✓ | ✓ | | ✓ | ✓ | | | ✓ | ✓ | ✓ | |

| | | | | | | | | | | | |
|---|---|---|---|---|---|---|---|---|---|---|---|
| 5. Make sure new buildings contribute to variety (through detail including colours, windows, roof tiling, as well as overall form) | ✓ | | ✓ | | ✓ | ✓ | | | | | |
| 6. Add special features (e.g. post boxes, telephone boxes, trees, statues) at junctions, particularly complex ones | ✓ | ✓ | | | ✓ | ✓ | | | ✓ | ✓ | |
| 7. Add porches, canopies and clear signs to make entrances to public buildings obvious | ✓ | ✓ | | | ✓ | ✓ | | | | ✓ | |
| 8. Increase the widths of footways (e.g. by reducing the widths of roads) | ✓ | ✓ | | ✓ | | | | | ✓ | ✓ | |
| 9. On busy roads, create a buffer zone between pedestrians and cars (e.g. through trees, grass verges) | ✓ | ✓ | | ✓ | | | | | ✓ | ✓ | |
| 10. Move cycle lanes from footways to roads | ✓ | ✓ | | ✓ | | | | | ✓ | ✓ | |
| 11. Increase the frequency of pedestrian crossings | | | | ✓ | | | | | ✓ | ✓ | |
| 12. Where there are steps, attempt to provide a slope or ramp (no more than 1 in 20) as well | ✓ | ✓ | | ✓ | | | | | ✓ | ✓ | ✓ |

*(Continued)*

**Table 10.1** [*Continued*].

| | Architects | Urban designers | Planners (development control) | Highway engineers | Private developers | Not-for-profit developers | Street furniture manufacturers | Maintenance departments | Access officers | Town centre managers | Property managers | Local residents |
|---|---|---|---|---|---|---|---|---|---|---|---|---|
| 13. Add handrails to steps or ramps, if they do not have them | | | | ✓ | | | | | ✓ | ✓ | ✓ | |
| 14. Fix clear signs and symbols (where existing ones are poor) to publicly accessible buildings, preferably perpendicular to walls | | | | | ✓ | ✓ | ✓ | ✓ | ✓ | ✓ | ✓ | |
| 15. Remove all unclear and unnecessary signs | | | | | ✓ | ✓ | | ✓ | ✓ | ✓ | ✓ | |
| 16. Replace all unclear road and directional signs with clear ones (i.e. those with large graphics and realistic symbols in clear contrast to the background, preferably dark lettering on a light background) – all directional signs should be single pointers | | | | | ✓ | ✓ | | ✓ | ✓ | ✓ | ✓ | |

| | | | | | | | | | | | |
|---|---|---|---|---|---|---|---|---|---|---|---|
| 17. Increase variety in the existing built form (e.g. by painting doors and windows different colours and adding details such as window boxes) | ✓ | | | ✓ | ✓ | ✓ | | ✓ | ✓ | ✓ | ✓ |
| 18. Only use seats, telephone boxes, bus shelters and toilets that are suitable for older people (see individual recommendations for details) | | | | | ✓ | ✓ | | | | ✓ | |
| 19. Replace gates and doors where necessary so they require no more than 2 kg of pressure to open and have lever handles | | | ✓ | ✓ | ✓ | ✓ | ✓ | ✓ | ✓ | ✓ | ✓ |
| 20. Improve audible cues at pedestrian crossings where necessary to increase crossing time | | ✓ | ✓ | | | ✓ | | | ✓ | ✓ | |
| 21. Replace cobbled, rough or patterned footways with smooth, plain ones | | ✓ | ✓ | ✓ | | ✓ | | ✓ | ✓ | ✓ | ✓ |
| 22. Reduce street clutter (e.g. boards, adverts, signs) | | ✓ | ✓ | ✓ | ✓ | ✓ | | ✓ | ✓ | ✓ | ✓ |
| 23. Increase the amount of street lighting where necessary | | ✓ | ✓ | ✓ | ✓ | ✓ | | ✓ | ✓ | ✓ | ✓ |

*(Continued)*

143

**Table 10.1** [*Continued*].

**Maintaining urban areas**

| | Architects | Urban designers | Planners (development control) | Highway engineers | Private developers | Not-for-profit developers | Street furniture manufacturers | Maintenance departments | Access officers | Town centre managers | Property managers | Local residents |
|---|---|---|---|---|---|---|---|---|---|---|---|---|
| 1. Repair damaged footways and roads | | | | ✓ | | | | ✓ | | ✓ | ✓ | |
| 2. Cut back hedges and trees | | | | ✓ | | | | ✓ | | ✓ | ✓ | ✓ |
| 3. Clean and sweep footways and roads regularly | | | | ✓ | | | | ✓ | | ✓ | ✓ | ✓ |
| 4. Remove litter frequently | | | | | | | | ✓ | | ✓ | ✓ | ✓ |

## HOW?

This section considers the different approaches to implementing the Streets for Life concept and suggests how the recommendations are best put into practice by the different bodies listed above.

### ALL OR NOTHING?

We think that Streets for Life are most likely to be achieved if all our recommendations are followed, whether for new urban areas or adaptations. However, we are not advocating an all or nothing approach. Each recommendation is of value in its own right in helping to create streets that are easy and enjoyable to use as we grow older in our neighbourhoods. The more recommendations that are followed the better, but use of any is beneficial for creating inclusive neighbourhoods. There are perhaps some that are more fundamental than others – some will be of benefit to nearly all older people while others are of particular benefit to those with dementia. In terms of having the widest relevance and potential benefit, we would tentatively rank the seventeen Streets for Life design features as follows (from the most to least important):

1. A mix of uses, including plenty of services and facilities and open space.
2. Wide, smooth, non-slip footways (without cycle lanes).
3. Frequent road crossings with audible and visual cues suitable for older people.
4. Clear signs throughout.
5. Frequent wooden seating, with arm and back rests.
6. Small blocks laid out on an irregular grid (with minimal crossroads).
7. Clearly marked level changes, with handrails.
8. Ground level toilets.
9. Enclosed bus shelters, with seating.
10. Varied urban form and architecture.
11. Busy routes with buffer zone between road and footway (e.g. trees, grass verge).
12. Landmarks, distinctive structures and places of activity.
13. A hierarchy of streets from main to side.
14. Special/distinctive features at junctions.
15. Buildings with obvious entrances.
16. Buildings designed to reflect uses.
17. Gently winding streets.

We put a mix of uses first because facilities, services and open space need to be within easy reach for those who often find walking difficult. Next, we have listed the recommendations that help older people to walk safely and

**Figure 10.3** A mix of uses is perhaps the most fundamental ingredient of Streets for Life.

comfortably to the places they want to visit – so, wide, smooth, non-slip foot-ways are very important, as are adequate seating, toilets and handrails. It is also important that older people can walk relatively directly to their destin-ations, through a street network that is well connected in a grid pattern – this gives them lots of choices of routes and avoids the lengthy walks and confu-sion often created by cul-de-sac patterns. The remaining recommendations are more relevant for people with dementia, helping them to find their way around. Their focus is ensuring variety in the environment and having plenty of landmarks and distinctive features.

The priorities will vary for the different professionals and groups of people responsible for creating and managing streets.

**Figure 10.4**   Wide, smooth footways are a key characteristic of Streets for Life.

## BACK TO PRINCIPLES

We feel it is important to say that our principles, criteria or objectives for designing Streets for Life are as important as our recommendations. The recommendations are drawn from just one research project focusing on a limited number
of older people – there may be many other ways of achieving the six principles of

familiarity, legibility, distinctiveness, accessibility, comfort and safety. We would encourage those wanting to create Streets for Life to look back at older people's needs and requirements when designing streets and neighbourhoods. We have developed specific recommendations because we feel these would be easy to use, particularly by designers, and because the older people we spoke to had fairly strong views about what they felt did and did not work for them in their environments. But we do not claim we have all the answers. This is original and early work in the field and we know there is a lot more to find out.

We are also conscious that we do not want to limit the creativity of designers. Good designers may well come up with new solutions. We have only made recommendations on the basis of how older people view the environments that are already around them. New solutions may be either built environment or technological ones.

So we suggest that both principles and recommendations, or either, are used in designing Streets for Life. We hope that over time we or other people will contribute more recommendations to the Streets for Life concept.

## SEAMLESS DESIGN FOR LIFE

Ideally, Streets for Life recommendations should be used alongside guidance for other aspects of lifetime design. There will be little advantage in older people being able to continue using their local streets if their homes are no longer suitable. Further, older people need transport, whether private or public, to be accessible and comfortable. And for a good quality of life they need open spaces and parks that are easy to enjoy. It is also important that they can enter and use shops, libraries, healthcare buildings, places of worship and other facilities. We intend the Streets for Life concept to form one important part of a whole new inclusive approach to design, from the armchair to the home, street and town centre beyond.

## PUTTING IT ALL TOGETHER

We realise that designers are faced with enormous challenges when designing outdoor environments because of the many different requirements placed on them. Urban environments are complex because they have so many different users and so many different uses, which change over time. It is not always possible to predict exactly how urban areas will be used – it will depend on the weather, the season, the time of day, on events that are happening and facilities and services that are in operation at any one time. There are many issues to consider when producing or maintaining streets and neighbourhoods, including:

- Conservation of heritage
- Environmental sustainability

- Needs of other users (e.g. those of different ages and abilities, visitors as well as residents)
- Designers' requirements (e.g. aesthetic objectives)
- Developers' requirements (e.g. cost, profitability, ease of maintenance).

We are not suggesting that the Streets for Life recommendations should override any others. Our recommendations obviously have to be considered along with other requirements, and it is possible there may be conflicts. The issues that take priority will vary from situation to situation.

We have tested our recommendations with a group of professionals responsible for creating urban environments to find out if there are problems with any of them (i.e. to see if they are feasible in terms of costs and practicality and if they conflict with other users' requirements). We only kept those recommendations that were seen to be of benefit to all users. However, they have yet to be tested in detail. They form guidance for just one aspect of sustainability. There is clearly further to go in looking at how far they contribute to achieving sustainable communities. We have already begun to pursue this through further research. We hope Streets for Life will be just one component of design guidance in the future – for sustainable communities and development in general.

# 11 CHAPTER

# Going further with Streets for Life

## INTRODUCTION

We have outlined what Streets for Life are and why we think they are needed (Part 1). We have also put forward a series of design recommendations that we believe will help achieve Streets for Life (Part 2). In Chapter 10 of Part 3, we explained how, where and by whom the recommendations are best implemented. What remains to say is where we go from here, what we think the Streets for Life concept and recommendations contribute, what the limitations are and what further work is needed in the future.

# FURTHER WORK

People have shown considerable enthusiasm for our Streets for Life concept and have been contacting us from around the world to find out about the recommendations. We have been very happy to help people and the huge interest shown was a spur to writing this book. However, we are also cautious, because the research has clear limitations. These are the main ones:

## REPRESENTATIVENESS OF RESEARCH

The Streets for Life recommendations are based on pioneering work using novel research methods. They are the outcome of just one piece of research using a sample of 45 older people with and without dementia. There is no doubt that we interviewed these people in depth, probing them about their local streets and neighbourhoods, and showing them photographs of lots of different aspects of street design. We also went out with them for walks in their neighbourhoods to see at first hand what helped and hampered them in getting about and enjoying themselves. So we are confident that we got to the bottom of their design concerns and what makes a difference to their quality of life. But, nevertheless, to feel truly confident, we need to talk to many more older people.

We are in the process of doing this now, through a project called I'DGO – Inclusive Design for Getting Outdoors (see the web site, at http://www.idgo. ac.uk). This is being funded again by the Engineering and Physical Sciences Research Council, and we are doing the work with the following partners:

- SURFACE Inclusive Design Research Centre, the University of Salford
- OPENspace Research Centre, Edinburgh College of Art/Heriot Watt University
- Research Institute for Consumer Affairs (RICAbility)
- Housing Corporation
- Dementia Voice
- Sensory Trust.

Through this project we are asking a further 200 older people about their local neighbourhood environments. We are also measuring and recording the design characteristics of their local neighbourhoods so that we can find out if people are more likely to give positive reports in particular types of neighbourhoods.

## DEPTH OF INFORMATION FOR INDIVIDUAL ASPECTS OF DESIGN

We have been deliberately broad in our research so far – we wanted to find out older people's views on all aspects of the design of outdoor environments.

**Figure 11.1**    We are investigating Streets for Life further through the I'DGO (Inclusive Design for Getting Outdoors) project, funded by EPSRC (2002–2006). (Photograph by Takemi Sugiyama, © OPENspace Research Centre.)

This has meant the research is comprehensive and gives us an idea of the aspects that are of most concern, but what we have not been able to do is to focus in depth on anything.

Depending on what we find in the I'DGO project, we are then planning to carry out further research on some individual aspects of the outdoor environment, to investigate them in more detail. For example, we may focus on older people's gardens and other private outdoor spaces, including balconies

**Figure 11.2** We still need to investigate in greater detail certain aspects of design, such as private outdoor space.

and terraces, to determine what older people value most in terms of their design. This will be particularly relevant as the UK government's urban renaissance policies and Sustainable Communities Plan strategies are requiring developers to build higher-density housing on previously used urban land. The arguments are that a large amount of new housing is required to accommodate the growing numbers of older people, and that these households, often older people living on their own, do not need a large amount of space. There is a danger that in these higher-density developments, private garden space will be lost. We feel it is important to find out how much value older people place on this outdoor space and to investigate, even if little land is available, how they would best like their garden space delivered – for example, are balconies an attractive alternative as they require less maintenance? There is also the issue of how private outdoor space should be provided for sheltered housing and care homes. If the space is shared among residents, what are the key ingredients that will make the space enjoyable to use for residents?

There is endless scope for research on further aspects of design: for example, the design of urban open spaces such as squares; or the design of smaller features such as public seats. We are hoping over time to cover as many facets of design as possible, to provide the depth and detail of information needed to create truly sustainable outdoor areas.

## SCALES/SETTINGS BEYOND THE NEIGHBOURHOOD

The Streets for Life recommendations include guidance for most aspects of design of the local neighbourhood, from the overall street network and urban form to detailing of footways and seats. However, they do not cover all outdoor settings, for example, open countryside, woods, country parks, National Trust properties and other leisure attractions. They also do not give detailed guidance on parks, squares and other large public spaces, although some of the recommendations are relevant for these settings.

We have not given advice at the broader scale for larger-scale regional and county planning, and strategic growth management. There may be questions about how population growth should be accommodated in the future, whether through urban extensions, satellite villages, developments of smaller towns around cities and so on. How choices about future development at this scale might affect older people's quality of life should be the subject of new research. Such choices may well be hugely significant for this section of the population, particularly in terms of access to services and facilities, and green space.

## INDIVIDUAL DIFFERENCES

We are aware that in formulating our Streets for Life recommendations, we have tried to find common threads, points of agreement among our participants, and general tendencies. What this masks, however, are the fairly significant differences among individual older people in their views of the outdoor environment. Obviously, street environments cannot be designed to suit individual preferences as they are used by a very wide range of people, so we have to find design characteristics that are seen by the majority to be beneficial. Streets for Life therefore may not serve everyone's needs. There are always going to be differences between people, not just because of their differing abilities and impairments, but also because of their personalities. There are those older people who value social interaction highly and are positive about any design features that allow them more opportunities to meet and chat to people, whereas there are those who value peace and quiet, and privacy above all else, and so are positive about the design features that support that. It is difficult to see a solution to this. It may be that personal technology and mobility aids could overcome some of the individual differences, or it might be that the outdoor environment could be designed to be more flexible and adaptable, capable of being used and appreciated in a variety of ways, to suit individuals. This is a new idea that needs further investigation and consideration.

## POTENTIAL CONFLICTS WITH OTHER USERS

An important limitation of our Streets for Life recommendations is that we have not looked in detail at possible conflicts with different users. We did test our preliminary findings with a group of professionals and designers involved in producing outdoor spaces, and dropped any recommendations that were felt to be problematic for other users, but we feel further work is needed to investigate the implications of Streets for Life recommendations for children, young people, parents with buggies or prams and people with sensory impairments. We would like Streets for Life to be places where children can play safely, where teenagers can meet and congregate without intimidating others and where people of all abilities can use and enjoy the outdoor environment. People use their streets for many different reasons, not just to get from A to B, but also to meet and talk, to walk their dogs, to exercise through running or jogging or to play. For Streets for Life to be properly inclusive, they need to accommodate all these uses alongside each other without difficulty.

## POTENTIAL CONFLICTS WITH OTHER TRANSPORT NEEDS

Our research has been limited so far to pedestrians – we have been interested in the experience of older people walking along and through their local streets. We have not investigated the needs of cyclists and car drivers, or examined whether or not the Streets for Life recommendations are detrimental in any way for them. In fact, to ensure a good quality of life for older households, ease of driving around their neighbourhoods is an important consideration. It may well be that the design characteristics required to deliver a good walking environment are not those, or even the opposite of those, that provide a good driving environment. This should be the subject of further research. We believe the walking environment should take priority however, simply because so many older people cannot drive, lose the ability to drive or do not have access to a car. None of the people with dementia we interviewed were able to continue driving, so their trips were limited to places to which they could comfortably walk.

**Figure 11.3**   Streets for Life need to be appropriate for all ages, not just older people.

We also realise that the quality and design of public transport, including the services, infrastructure and vehicles, are important concerns for older people. Many continue to use, or begin to use, public transport as they get older. Although we have looked at bus shelters (as aspects of street furniture),

**Figure 11.4**   There may be conflicts between the needs of pedestrians and the needs of cyclists.

we have not looked at vehicles, services or wider infrastructure. There are experts in transport who are addressing these issues, or at least are likely to address them over the next few years.

## POTENTIAL CONFLICTS WITH OTHER SUSTAINABILITY REQUIREMENTS

Sustainability covers a wide range of issues, within the three broad categories of social, environmental and economic sustainability. The Streets for Life recommendations contribute mainly to the social aspects of sustainability, because they aim to improve people's quality of life and make places more accessible for

**Figure 11.5** Streets for Life are walkable streets; sustainability objectives require them to support public transport too.

everyone. A socially sustainable environment is said to have the following characteristics (Burton, 2000; 2003):

- Provides good quality of life for all
- Is accessible (everybody can use it)
- Is safe (from traffic and crime)
- Is easy and pleasant to walk around
- Has plenty of services, facilities and open space.

These tie in well with Streets for Life. Environmental sustainability is concerned mainly with reducing energy use, conserving resources and limiting pollution. A primary goal is to encourage people to walk, cycle and use public transport rather than private cars. The Streets for Life recommendations clearly support this goal. There may be other environmental goals, however, that are difficult to achieve by following the recommendations. For example, providing energy through solar panels requires a lower-density urban form, which might make facilities difficult to reach for older people. Further study is needed to examine potential conflicts with environmental and economic sustainability, but on the whole the recommendations appear to support sustainable development.

## PRACTICAL AND ECONOMIC FEASIBILITY

This is an area we haven't explored in depth. If incorporated early on in the design process when creating new or redeveloped urban areas, the recommendations appear unlikely to imply any additional cost. However, costs would need to be incurred to bring existing urban areas in line with the Streets for Life concept. Some of the costs would not be significant, for example, painting doors, windows, walls and gates to increase variety (especially if this forms part of ongoing maintenance). We would like to analyse the economic feasibility of Streets for Life for future promotion of the idea. Watch this space!

## POTENTIAL CONFLICTS WITH DESIGNERS' REQUIREMENTS

This is the area we were perhaps most concerned about when presenting our findings to designers. The recommendations might be difficult to apply for two reasons:

1. Designers do not have the time or mechanisms to incorporate this guidance, alongside all their other requirements.
2. Designers may feel their creativity will be repressed, or the recommendations conflict with artistic/aesthetic concerns.

We are addressing the first difficulty through the I'DGO project mentioned earlier. One part of this project is to survey designers and other producers of outdoor environments through a questionnaire to find out what they know already about designing for older people, what they would like to know, and their preferences for the form and content of any guidance. We are hoping to use the findings from this questionnaire to develop new guidance from the I'DGO research.

We have had a good response to our Streets for Life findings from a range of architects, urban designers and local planning authorities, but we feel there may be some professionals who will interpret them as ruling out anything 'modern'. We have been careful not to say that older people always prefer 'traditional' designs – instead, we say that older people like uses and functions to be clear and recognisable. If a church looks like a church (maybe because it has a steeple) even though it is modern in design, then that is fine for Streets for Life. Older people, like all groups of people, have widely different views on what they like and don't like when it comes to aesthetics. It would be impossible for us to recommend any particular style of design. So, this leaves a lot of scope for designers. The recommendations are not prescriptive in terms of aesthetics. Limiting footway surfaces to smooth, plain materials may be seen to be restrictive, but interest can be created in other ways, for example, through planters, lighting and decorative features. It would be useful to have further feedback from designers on their views of the recommendations.

## THE CONTRIBUTION OF STREETS FOR LIFE

### UNDERSTANDING OLDER PEOPLE'S USE AND PERCEPTION OF THEIR OUTDOOR ENVIRONMENTS

Before this Wellbeing in Sustainable Environments (WISE) research, no one had investigated older people's perceptions of individual design features of their outdoor environments, and no one had interviewed people with dementia about their neighbourhoods. We now know much more about why, how and when older people go out, how they feel when they are out and what their main design concerns are (Burton and Mitchell, 2003). We also know the main differences in perceptions for those with and without dementia. This is valuable information that can be used by a variety of people for a range of different purposes. Not only can it be used as the basis for design guidance, it can also be used by those responsible for managing public transport, and by those involved in community activities.

### ENHANCEMENT OF OLDER PEOPLE'S QUALITY OF LIFE

The ultimate aim of our research and the Streets for Life recommendations is to improve the quality of life of older people. When we devise principles of good urban design, their objective is usually to improve people's quality of life in some way, or to increase users' levels of enjoyment or satisfaction. For people with dementia, however, appropriate urban design can achieve much more than this – it is fundamental to their survival, sense of worth and self-esteem. Indeed, it directly affects whether or not, and how often, they go out. There is a growing need to consider the implications of ageing in urban design. The design for dementia literature concentrates on the internal design of institutions; guidance on the design of the outdoor environment beyond the boundaries of facilities is almost non-existent. The literature, however, suggests that the internal design principles are having a positive effect on the functional and cognitive abilities of residents.

Our research is beginning to show that the outdoor environment can be designed to help older people with dementia to identify and understand

**Figure 11.6**  Enjoying the outdoor environment is central to older people's quality of life.

where they are, to make appropriate behavioural and wayfinding decisions, to feel safe and comfortable and to access and use their local neighbourhoods. The research focuses on the needs of a relatively small, but rapidly growing, section of society yet the design issues raised are also important for older people in general and for many other people with sensory, cognitive or physical impairments. Furthermore, designing for longevity and creating dementia-friendly neighbourhoods will be of benefit to society as a whole.

## ENABLING OLDER PEOPLE TO REMAIN INDEPENDENT AND 'STAY PUT'

The general consensus among older people, policy-makers, health professionals and service providers is that it is best if older people can stay living in their own homes, and remain independent, as long as possible. This is best because it:

- Is what older people want
- Reduces the need for public spending
- Reduces pressure on care homes, which are in limited supply
- Is good for the health of older people, especially those with dementia.

Streets for Life can help older people 'stay put'. Neighbourhoods built or adapted to Streets for Life recommendations or principles enable older people to continue going out, using their local facilities and meeting people in the neighbourhood. Unless they can do this, their quality of life, whether at home or not, is severely limited.

## INCLUSIVE DESIGN

Streets for Life contribute towards creating environments that are accessible for all. We have been careful to select recommendations that appear to be beneficial for all members of society, whatever their age, ability or gender. Although there has been some development in furthering an inclusive design agenda for products and homes, there has been relatively little attention given to the idea of inclusive urban design. We hope these recommendations will go some way towards filling this gap.

## SUSTAINABLE COMMUNITIES

Sustainable communities are ones that provide a good quality of life for all, and accessible, safe environments that encourage walking and cycling. Streets for Life are clearly sustainable. They contribute mainly towards social aspects of sustainability, but also environmental ones by enabling people to walk and cycle rather than drive to facilities.

## METHODS FOR FURTHER RESEARCH ON PEOPLE
## AND THEIR ENVIRONMENT

We were amazed by the quality of information we were able to obtain from older people with dementia. Very often dementia-related research involves interviews with carers, relatives and friends or health professionals involved in the care of people with dementia, believing that it is impossible or impractical to interview those with dementia themselves. We have proved this wrong. Not only did older people with dementia generally really enjoy taking part in the research, feeling their views were valued, but they also showed an ability to contribute interesting, clear answers to our questions.

We hope that the methods we have developed will be of use to other researchers in obtaining the views and perceptions of people with dementia. We always telephoned ahead on interview days to check the state of mind of participants – they can have good and bad days, and if necessary we postponed interviews to wait for a 'good' day. Our questionnaire was an in-depth semi-structured one – it did not matter if the participants wanted to answer the questions in a different order, or skip backwards and forwards. We made sure we recorded their statements so we had time to interpret them carefully later (people with dementia tend to talk in metaphors). We used sets of photographs to aid the discussion – people with dementia struggle to talk about abstract concepts, so commenting on pictures in front of them was easier than giving views of general issues. We found the accompanied walks to be of great use – often people with dementia forget how and why they use outdoor environments, but going on trips with them enabled us to ask why they had gone a particular way or how they had known which way to go. There was a lot about the design of the environment that we found out from the walks that we could not have uncovered in interviews.

We also developed a checklist for measuring the design characteristics of people's local neighbourhoods. We used this in statistical analyses to see if participants' use/enjoyment of their environments was related to particular design features. We have used a similar checklist in other research projects and believe it provides a novel, valuable way of examining the impacts of built environments on people's lives (Weich *et al.*, 2001; Burton *et al.*, 2005).

## A SHIFT IN ATTITUDES TO DESIGNING URBAN AREAS

Finally, we hope Streets for Life will play a small part in bringing about a shift in attitudes towards the design of our environments. I trained as an architect in the 1980s. Then, as now, we were taught to be creative and original. We read very little – our study was almost wholly studio-based. Research for designing a building consisted of visiting the site and getting a 'feel' for the place. We might have investigated practical requirements for the building and perhaps interviewed a mock client. In the public defence of our student schemes ('crits'), the worst reason we could give for designing the way we had was that it was 'what people liked'. Buildings were viewed as pieces of sculpture rather than environments accommodating people.

Perhaps this attitude was a reaction to the so-called architectural determinism of the Modern era. Architects had been criticised for social engineering – trying to mould people to behave in certain ways. But I felt there must be a middle ground. As architects and urban designers, we have a social responsibility. People can generally choose whether or not to view works of art such as paintings and sculptures, and it does not really matter if they hate them. But we are creating homes, buildings, neighbourhoods and town centres people have to live and work in, places they grow up in and grow old in, the settings for discovery, relationships and activity. The evidence is showing that environments matter; they do have significant influences on people's lives – their opportunities, quality of life and their emotional and physical wellbeing (e.g. Weich *et al.*, 2002).

When medical doctors treat their patients, they use only drugs and treatments that have been properly tried and tested – they know what effects they will have. Why should it be different for the environments we deliver? Surely we should do our best to find out what works and what does not for people, identifying the best of what has already been built as a basis from which to move forward. If we have an understanding of the basic principles (people's requirements in terms of design and how different design features affect these) then we have the knowledge and tools for designing environments that enhance people's lives. We still need creativity. We still need inspiration and good ideas, but there is a framework on which to build. We can create new and modern designs that still satisfy people's requirements – if we know what the key ingredients are. What is it about people's favourite places that make them so? We have a long way to go in answering this, but the WISE research unit has made a start. Its long-term goal is to provide information from which designers can produce socially responsible design.

Community participation in design has been put forward as a way of addressing user needs. However, there are several difficulties with this, especially at the scale of the street or neighbourhood:

- those with the loudest voices tend to get the most attention – their views may not be representative
- the needs of the existing community may not be those of future ones
- the needs/views of the least advantaged, most excluded members of society tend to be overlooked
- local communities do not necessarily know what is possible in terms of design – they do not have the advantage of design training

- streets and neighbourhoods have a wide and complex range of uses and users – local communities may not consider the needs of them all, especially visitors and those working rather than living in neighbourhoods
- local communities may not necessarily consider wider objectives such as the needs of society as a whole (e.g. the need for affordable housing) or environmental issues.

We therefore call for a different approach to design – one that uses the creativity and skill of the designer but draws on knowledge of what users need or want and evidence of what is and is not successful in terms of this. There needs to be a subtle shift in practice and, importantly, a bigger shift in education. Architects often view evidence as pragmatic and uninspiring. We believe the opposite – we believe Streets for Life and other user-centred, research-based design guidance can lead to a brighter, better future for our towns and cities. Streets for Life is a vision, one that can bring greater sustainability, wellbeing and hope.

# Bibliography

AIA (American Institute of Architects) (1985). *Design for Aging: An Architect's Guide.* Washington, DC: AIA Press.

Alzheimer's Association (2000). *People with Alzheimer's disease.* Available at: http://www.alz.org

Alzheimer's Society (2000). *About dementia. Statistics.* Available at: http://www.alzheimers.org.uk/about/statistics/html

Audit Commission (2000). *Forget me not: mental health services for older people.* Available at: http://www.audit-commission.gov.uk

Australian Government (1992). *Disability Discrimination Act.* Available at: http://www.comlaw.gov.au.comlaw/legislation/actcompilation1.nsf/current/bytitle/E158A29AF9

Axia, G., Peron, E. and Baroni, M. (1991). Environmental assessment across the life span. In *Environment, Cognition and Action: An Integrated Approach* (T. Garling and G. Evans, eds) pp. 221–244. Oxford: Oxford University Press.

Baragwanath, A. (1997). Bounce and balance: a team approach to risk management for people with dementia living at home. In *State of the Art in Dementia Care* (M. Marshall, ed.) pp. 102–105. London: Centre for Policy on Ageing.

Barberger-Gateau, P. and Fabrigoule, C. (1997). Disability and cognitive impairment in the elderly. *Disability and Rehabilitation*, **19(5)**, 175–193.

Barker, P. and Fraser, J. (1999). *Sign Design Guide: A Guide to Inclusive Signage.* London: JMU Access Partnership and Harpenden Sign Design Society.

Barnett Waddingham (2002). *The ageing population – burden or benefit?* Available at: http://www.barnett-waddingham.co.uk/cms/services/inscomps/news02023/view-document

Brawley, E. (1997). *Designing for Alzheimer's Disease: Strategies for Creating Better Care Environments.* New York: John Wiley.

Brawley, E. (2001). Environmental design for Alzheimer's disease: a quality of life issue. *Aging and Mental Health*, **5(Suppl 1)**, S79–S83.

Brewerton, J. and Darton, D. (eds) (1997). *Designing Lifetime Homes*. York: Joseph Rowntree Foundation.

Burley, R. and Pollock, R. (1992). *Every House You'll Ever Need: Designing Out Disorientation in the Home*. Stirling: Dementia Services Development Centre.

Burton, E. (2000). The compact city: just or just compact? A preliminary analysis. *Urban Studies*, **37(11)**, 1969–2006.

Burton, E. (2002). Measuring urban compactness in UK towns and cities. *Environment and Planning B*, **29(2)**, 219–250.

Burton, E. (2003). Housing for an urban renaissance: implications for social equity. *Housing Studies*, **18(4)**, 537–562.

Burton, E. and Mitchell, L. (2003). Urban design for longevity: designing dementia-friendly neighbourhoods. *Urban Design Quarterly*, **87**, 32–35.

Burton, E., Mitchell, L. and Raman, S. (2004). *Neighbourhoods for Life: Designing Dementia-Friendly Outdoor Environments. A Findings Leaflet*. Oxford: Oxford Institute for Sustainable Development, Oxford Brookes University.

Burton, E., Weich, S., Blanchard, M. and Prince, M. (2005). Measuring physical characteristics of housing: the Built Environment Site Survey Checklist (BESSC). *Environment and Planning B*, **32(2)**, 265–280.

CABE (Commission for Architecture and the Built Environment) (2005). *Better Neighbourhoods: Making Higher Densities Work*. London: CABE.

Calkins, M. (1988). *Design for Dementia: Planning Environments for the Elderly and the Confused*. Owings Mills, MD: National Health Publishing.

Campbell, S. (2005). *Deteriorating Vision, Falls and Older People: The Links*. Glasgow: Visibility.

Carroll, C., Cowans, J. and Darton, D. (eds) (1999). *Meeting Part M and Designing Lifetime Homes*. York: Joseph Rowntree Foundation.

Carstens, D. (1985). *Site Planning and Design for the Elderly: Issues, Guidelines and Alternatives*. New York: Van Nostrand Reinhold.

Cornell, E., Heth, C. and Skoczylas, M. (1999). The nature and use of route expectations following incidental learning. *Journal of Environmental Psychology*, **19**, 209–229.

DETR (Department of the Environment, Transport and the Regions) (1998). *Planning for the Communities of the Future*. London: The Stationery Office.

DETR (Department of the Environment, Transport and the Regions) (1999). *Quality of Life Counts: Indicators for a Strategy for Sustainable Development for the United Kingdom*. London: The Stationery Office.

DETR (Department of the Environment, Transport and the Regions) (2000a). *Our Towns and Cities: The Future – Delivering an Urban Renaissance*. London: Stationery Office.

DETR (Department of the Environment, Transport and the Regions) (2000b). *Planning Policy Guidance 3: Housing (revised)*. London: The Stationery Office.

DETR and CABE (Department of the Environment, Transport and the Regions and Commission for Architecture and the Built Environment) (2000). *By Design. Urban Design in the Planning System: Towards Better Practice*. London: The Stationery Office.

DETR and DoH (Department of the Environment, Transport and the Regions and Department of Health) (2001). *Quality and Change for Older People's Housing: A Strategic Framework*. London: The Stationery Office.

DfEE (Department for Education and Employment) (2001). *Towards Inclusion: Civil Rights for Disabled People. Government Response to the Disability Rights Task Force*. London: The Stationery Office.

DoE (Department of the Environment) (1996). *Planning Policy Guidance 6: Town Centres and Retail Development (revised)*. London: HMSO.

DoE and DoT (Department of the Environment and Department of Transport) (1994). *Planning Policy Guidance 13: Transport*. London: HMSO.

DSDC (Dementia Services Development Centre) (1995). *Dementia in the Community: Management Strategies for General Practice*. London: Alzheimer's Disease Society.

DTLR (Department of Transport, Local Government and the Regions) (2001). *By Design. Better Places to Live: A Companion Guide to PPG3*. London: The Stationery Office.

Fabisch, G. (2003). Meeting the needs of elderly and disabled people in standards. Paper given at the *European Standards Bodies Conference, Accessibility for All*, European Standards Organisations: CEN, CENELEC and ETSI, 27–28 March 2003, Nice, France.

Faletti, M. (1984). Human factors research and functional environments for the aged. In *Elderly People and the Environment. Human Behaviour and Environment: Advances in Theory and Research, Vol. 7* (I. Altman, M. Powell Lawton and J. Wohlwill, eds) pp. 191–237. New York: Plenum Press.

Fogel, B. (1992). Psychological aspects of staying at home. *Journal of the American Society on Aging*, **16(2)**, 15–27.

Gant, R. (1997). Pedestrianisation and disabled people: a study of personal mobility in Kingston town centre. *Disability and Society*, **12(5)**, 723–740.

Goldsmith, M. (1996). *Hearing the Voice of People with Dementia: Opportunities and Obstacles*. London: Jessica Kingsley.

Golledge, R. (1991). Cognition of physical and built environments. In *Environment, Cognition and Action: An Integrated Approach* (T. Garling and G. Evans, eds) pp. 35–62. Oxford: Oxford University Press.

Greenberg, L. (1982). The implication of an ageing population for land-use planning. In *Geographical Perspectives on the Elderly* (A. Warnes, ed.) pp. 401–425. Chichester: John Wiley.

Hall, P. and Imrie, R. (1999). Architectural practices and disabling design in the built environment. *Environment and Planning B – Planning and Design*, **26(3)**, 409–425.

Harrington, T. (1993). *Perception and Physiological Psychology in Designing for Older People with Cognitive and Affective Disorders*. Eindhoven: Institute for Gerontology, University of Eindhoven.

Help the Aged (2005a). *Age discrimination*. Available at: http://www.helptheaged. org.uk/CampaignNews/AgeDiscrimination/_default.htm

Help the Aged (2005b). *Incontinence*. Available at: http://www.helptheaged.org.uk/ Health/Conditions/Incontinence/default.htm

Help the Aged (2005c). *About us*. Available at: http://www.helptheaged.org.uk/_boiler-plate/About+Us/default.htm

Hillman, J. (1990). The importance of the street. *Town and Country Planning*, February, 42–46.

HM Government (1994). *Sustainable Development: The UK Strategy*, Cm 2426. London: HMSO.

Housing Corporation (2002). *Housing for Older People*. London: Housing Corporation.

Housing Corporation (2003). *Affordable Housing: Better by Good Design*. London: Housing Corporation.

Huppert, F. and Wilcock, G. (1997). Ageing, cognition and dementia. *Age and Ageing*, **26-S4**, 20–23.

Imrie, R. (2001). *Inclusive Design: Designing and Developing Accessible Environments*. London: Spon.

Imrie, R. and Kumar, M. (1998). Focusing on disability and access in the built environment. *Disability and Society*, **13(3)**, 357–374.

Kalasa, B. (2001). Population and ageing in Africa: a policy dilemma? *Conference proceedings of the XXIV General Conference of the International Union for the Scientific Study of Population*, Brazil, 18–24 August.

Kitchin, R. (2000). Collecting and analysing cognitive mapping data. In *Cognitive Mapping: Past, Present and Future* (R. Kitchin and S. Freundschuh, eds) pp. 9–23. London: Routledge.

Lacey, A. (2004). *Designing for Accessibility: Inclusive Environments*. London: RIBA Enterprises and Centre for Accessible Environments.

Laing and Buisson (2005). Available at: http://www.laingbuisson.co.uk

Lavery, I., Davey, S., Woodside, A. and Ewart, K. (1996). The vital role of street design and management in reducing barriers to older people's mobility. *Landscape and Urban Planning*, **35(2–3)**, 181–192.

Laws, G. (1994). Aging, contested meanings, and the built environment. *Environment and Planning A*, **26**, 1787–1802.

Lipman, P. (1991). Age and exposure differences in the acquisition of route information. *Psychology and Aging* **(6)**, 128–133.

Llewelyn-Davies (2000). *Urban Design Compendium*. London: Llewelyn-Davis.

Lubinski, R. (1991). Learned helplessness: application to communication of the elderly. In *Dementia and Communication* (R. Lubinski, ed.) pp. 142–151. San Diego, CA: Singular Publishing Group.

Lynch, K. (1960). *The Image of the City*. Cambridge, MA: MIT Press.

Marshall, M. (1998). A brighter horizon. *Community Care Supplement: Inside Dementia*, 29 October–4 November, 2–3.

Mitchell, L. and Burton, E. (2004). *Neighbourhoods for Life: A Checklist of Recommendations for Designing Dementia-Friendly Outdoor Environments*. Oxford: Housing Corporation and Oxford Brookes University.

Mitchell, L., Burton, E., Raman, S., Blackman, T., Jenks, M. and Williams, K. (2003). Making the outside world dementia friendly: design issues and considerations. *Environment and Planning B – Planning and Design*, **30(4)**, 605–632.

Moore, G. (1991). Life-span developmental issues on environmental assessment, cognition, and action: applications to environmental policy, planning and design. In *Environment, Cognition and Action: An Integrated Approach* (T. Garling and G. Evans, eds) pp. 309–331. Oxford: Oxford University Press.

National Statistics Online (2002). *Census 2001. Population report: demographics*. Available at: http://www.statistics.gov.uk/census2001/demographic_uk.asp

Norman, A. (1987). *Aspects of Ageism: A Discussion Paper*. London: Centre for Policy on Ageing.

ODPM (Office of the Deputy Prime Minister) (2003). *Sustainable Communities: Building for the Future*. London: The Stationery Office.

ODPM (Office of the Deputy Prime Minister) (2005a). *Planning Policy Statement 1: Delivering Sustainable Development*. London: The Stationery Office.

ODPM (Office of the Deputy Prime Minister) (2005b). *Excluded Older People: Social Exclusion Unit Interim Report*. London: The Stationery Office.

ODPM/CABE (2000). *By Design – Urban Design in the Planning System: Towards Better Practice*. London: The Stationery Office.

Oxley, P. (2002). *Inclusive Mobility. A Guide to Best Practice on Access to Pedestrian and Transport Infrastructure*. London: The Stationery Office.

Passini, R., Rainville, C., Marchand, N. and Joanette, Y. (1998). Wayfinding and dementia: some research findings and a new look at design. *Journal of Architectural and Planning Research*, **15(2)**, 133–151.

Passini, R., Pigot, H., Rainville, C. and Tetreault, M.-H. (2000). Wayfinding in a nursing home for advanced dementia of the Alzheimer's type. *Environment and Behaviour*, **32(5)**, 684–710.

Patoine, B. and Mattoli, S. (2001). *Staying Sharp: Current Advances in Brain Research. Memory Loss and Aging*. Washington, DC: AARP Andrus Foundation, and New York: the Dana Alliance for Brain Initiatives.

Peace, S. (1982). The activity patterns of elderly people in Swansea, South Wales, and south-east England. In *Geographical Perspectives on the Elderly* (A. Warnes, ed.) pp. 281–301. Chichester: John Wiley.

Perrin, T. and May, H. (2000). *Wellbeing in Dementia: An Occupational Approach for Therapists and Carers*. Edinburgh: Churchill Livingstone.

Reisberg, B., Ferris, S., Franssen, E., Kluger, A. and Borenstein, J. (1986). Age-associated memory impairment: the clinical syndrome. *Developmental Neuropsychology*, **2(4)**, 401–412.

Robson, P. (1982). Patterns of activity and mobility among the elderly. In *Geographical Perspectives on the Elderly* (A. Warnes, ed.) pp. 265–280. Chichester: John Wiley and Sons.

Twining, C. (1991). *The Memory Handbook*. Bicester: Winslow Press Ltd.

United Kingdom Government (2005). *Disability Discrimination Act*. London: The Stationery Office.

United Nations (1999). *Population ageing 1999*. Available at: http://www.un.org/esa/population/publications/aging99/a99peu.txt

Urban Task Force (1999). *Towards an Urban Renaissance*. Final report of the Urban Task Force chaired by Lord Rogers. London: Urban Task Force.

US Department of Justice (1990). *Americans with Disabilities Act*. Available at: http://www.usdoj.gov/crt/ada/adahom1.htm

Weich, S., Burton, E., Blanchard, M., Prince, M., Sproston, K. and Erens, R. (2001). Measuring the built environment: validity of a site survey instrument for use in urban settings. *Health and Place*, **7**, 283–292.

Weich, S., Blanchard, M., Prince, M., Burton, E., Sproston, K. and Erens, R. (2002). Mental health and the built environment: a cross-sectional survey of individual and contextual risk factors for depression. *British Journal of Psychiatry*, **180**, 428–433.

WHO (World Health Organisation) (2004). *World Health Organisation launches new initiative to address the health needs of a rapidly ageing population.* Available at: http://www.who.int/mediacentre/news/releases/2004/pr60/en/

Wilkniss, S., Jones, M., Korol, D., Gold, P. and Manning, C. (1997). Age-related differences in an ecologically based study of route learning. *Psychology and Aging*, **12**, 372–375.

Wylde, M. (1998). *It's still time for universal design. Critical issues in aging, fall.* Available at: http://www.asaging.org/am/cia2/design.html

Zimring, C. and Gross, M. (1991). Searching for the environment in environmental cognition research. In *Environment, Cognition and Action: An Integrated Approach* (T. Garling and G. Evans, eds) pp. 78–95. Oxford: Oxford University Press.

# Index

Learning Resources
Centre